1970

This book may be kept

FEN DAYS

The Existentialist
Prolegomena

Frederick Sontag

The Existentialist Prolegomena
To a Future Metaphysics

The University of Chicago Press
Chicago and London

Library of Congress Catalog Card Number: 69-11315

The University of Chicago Press, Chicago 60637
The University of Chicago Press, Ltd., London W.C. 1

For V.C.F. and V.L.F.

Love vaunteth not itself . . .
First Corinthians 13:4

Preface

The Prologue and chapter 1 both tell something of the origin and evolution of this work. To try to recount that history in full, or to acknowledge all the assistance along the way, would be too long a task for a mere Preface. The present work was at least ten years in the making, and in that sense a full account of its evolution would amount to the intellectual autobiography of its author. The present volume is much different from its first draft, and each addition and change has a story behind it. For the reader, however, this is all beside the point, since the work as it finally appears in print must exist on its own. Either it has achieved an internal integrity and can stand alone and be so interpreted, or the author has failed.

Partly for this reason I will not try to thank publicly all those who have shown an interest in or made suggestions for this work along its way. Every author owes many debts, and, at least upon occasion, it may be best to leave these unspoken. Specifically, however, I must thank the Rockefeller Foundation for the invitation to be its guest at the Villa Serbelloni, Belaggio, Italy. During that time as a scholar in residence in the spring of 1967, I completed the major revisions which resulted in this present draft. My thanks also go to my typist in Rome during my sabbatical year there, Mrs. Joseph A. DeLia.

Politically we seem to be living in an age of fundamental challenge to every inherited tradition, and socially our generation accepts no convention without question. Philosophically and theologically we also are once again investigating first principles, and so this work comes at a time which is very receptive to metaphysical inquiry. If we are to find any intellectual stability today, it may have to be by building up a new metaphysical foundation for ourselves. Certainly, security in thought cannot now be achieved by assuming old procedures.

Parts of chapter 6 originally appeared in the October, 1967 issue of *The Journal of Religion* and in the March, 1964 issue of *Philosophy and Phenomenological Research*. Parts of chapter 7 appeared in an earlier version in the May, 1964 issue of the *Modern Schoolman*. Chapter 8 was originally presented to the XVIth International Congress of Philosophy held in 1963 in Mexico City. Permission to reprint portions of these as parts of these chapters is gratefully acknowledged.

In a time of frantic change, those to whom this book is dedicated stand as an amazing example that it is possible to adapt to new situations, to remain always young, and yet never to abandon principles simply for the sake of change or to gain momentary popularity. Such personal stability surely is the human origin of all theoretical metaphysics.

FREDERICK SONTAG

Claremont, California

Contents

Prologue

The birth of a philosophical work ought not to be an easy affair. If the structures which philosophy seeks to make plain were obvious, the philosopher's task would have been completed long ago. If the words conveying what he has seen could be chosen easily, writing would be less than a painful task. Yet a scarcity of words does not seem to be our current problem; the extant writings of philosophers, their commentators, and their historians cover more pages than any man can read; and still we are perplexed. For this reason, the main question in the mind of any author ought to be: Why do I write? What leads me to the words I use and to the formation of the concepts I employ? What can these hope to accomplish that others have not already done?

In the present instance, both Kant and Kierkegaard forced me to write. The attempt to answer Kant by placing existentialist ideas within his thought structure slowly molded both the concepts and my words, and the basis for a contemporary revival of metaphysical construction was the not inconsiderable goal set before me. Some years ago, while teaching Kierkegaard to one group with my left hand and Kant's *Prolegomena* to another with my right, I ignored the biblical injunction and began to try to work the two together. Stated ever so simply, it seemed to me that Kierkegaard's literary and psychological writings had actually provided the empirical basis for metaphysics which Kant had demanded to have shown to him before he could license any new metaphysical construction.

Yet, if mere ideas were printed sentences, all thinkers would be authors. Somehow the idea suggested itself that I should replace the key Kantian terms with the central existentialist concepts, and the first result of this effort was a "translation" of Kant's *Prolegomena*. That product seemed to me to contain interesting ideas, but they were bound up in a nearly unintelligible form, considering the distance of our age from Kant's. If you tamper with a structure such as Kant's, you learn the tensile strength of really great thought and you also encounter its resistance to change.

A second draft was attempted that tried, somewhat unsuccessfully, to improve the clarity. Finally, it became evident that nothing would do but to form a new structure for the new ideas. The attempt to parallel Kant's form was, in that sense, a failure and had to be abandoned. An entirely new essay was next written, drawn from the material produced by the first two efforts.

All that is here is the result of following the principle that being a philosopher means to become adept in the art of receiving and employing mental suggestion. Chapter 8, the concluding essay, is an idea generated by my reading of Heidegger's comments on Kant and metaphysics; it seemed both necessary to consider Heidegger an existential prolegomenist and to attempt the urgent task of putting his insights into a somewhat clearer form. Chapters 1–4 all resulted directly from the attempt to "translate" Kant, that is, to convert his thought structure to purposes other than his own and to do this by introducing new (existential) material. I was finally forced to abandon Kant's form in the third draft of this manuscript, thus releasing the ideas produced in the process of translation to speak for themselves in their own style.

Kant and Kierkegaard, whatever their contemporary influence, actually lived and wrote at some distance from our time. Sartre, Heidegger, and Wittgenstein, on the other hand, are very much a part of our present age. Chapter 5 attempts to distill from Sartre his insights into the importance of nothingness and to take from Heidegger his stress upon time as the central concept for

Part One

The Development of Prolegomena

1

An Existentialist Prolegomenon to a Future Metaphysics

The Foundation of Theology

Theology in the contemporary western world, and to that extent Christianity in general, has not had a completely adequate or acceptable metaphysical foundation since the work of Kant. That great thinker admittedly "found it necessary to deny knowledge, in order to make room for *faith*." [1] Although it is possible for the religious life to go on without such rational supports, the history of the churches since that time has often been a story of increasing insecurity, a decline of inner vitality, and a lack of powerful external proclamation. Undoubtedly many historical reasons help to account for this phenomenon; but, intellectually speaking, the wholesale turn of philosophy away from metaphysics is surely one of the most significant causes. Since Kant's time, philosophers have sometimes been interested in religion, but seldom has this taken the form of technical theology in the classical sense. The absence of such large-scale metaphysical construction has limited philosophy's interest in religion to the peripheral areas, e.g., ethics and politics.

If philosophy can be said to have gone its secular way because of its disbelief in the validity of metaphysics, such a thesis must

---

[1] Immanuel Kant, *Critique of Pure Reason,* Preface to the Second Edition, Bxxxi, translated by N. K. Smith (New York: Humanities Press, 1950) , p. 29.

account for Hegel and other nineteenth- and twentieth-century metaphysicians. It is historical fact that Hegelian metaphysics held almost unchallenged sway over our philosophical life at the beginning of the twentieth century. Yet Hegel's views, as the term 'idealist' reveals, often had their roots far from ordinary experience. Their basis was 'reason' alone, and the dialectic was couched in such complicated terminology as to make it appear essentially unrelated to the religious life and, in fact, to ordinary life in general.

Other metaphysicians have also appeared to break the metaphysical drought inaugurated by Kant, which was reinforced by the eventual wholesale revolt against Hegelian unreality. Yet somehow none have been able to redirect the course of philosophy toward metaphysics with the same force Kant and Hegel used to turn it away (Kant directly; Hegel by inducing an eventual negative reaction). Hegel grounded metaphysics in the abstract life of Reason, but apparently not in immediate experience. Existentialism, it is true, can be traced to certain Hegelian inspirations, but still, in the minds of its authors, it is primarily a revolt against him.

Philosophy of science and mathematical logic have developed rapidly as new movements within philosophy since the time of Kant. Both are significant and solidly based, but neither provides by nature any ground for reestablishing philosophy's pre-Kantian (i.e., metaphysical) relationship with either technical theology or with religion in general. Aside from these two closely associated areas of science and logic, little else of significance has arisen to turn philosophy forcefully from its acquired secularism —except existentialism. Unfortunately, however, this important and provocative movement has grown up as much outside philosophy as within it. The revolt against philosophy's current state has been staged almost more within the world of literature (e.g., by Camus and Unamuno) than inside philosophy's own technical province.

Nineteenth-century German thought was uniformly developed by academic philosophers; existentialism, in contrast, has been the product of men not formally within the philosophers' union. Partly for this reason, and partly owing to its iconoclastic nature and its love for unusual modes of expression, existentialism has never yet made its full impact felt within professional philosophy. These estranged camps must be reconciled so that the impact of existentialist discoveries can be felt by systematic philosophy as well as by theology. We need not all go so far as to become academic professors, but existentialism needs the discipline of at least the Socratic dedication to teaching as a profession.

The advocates of existentialism often speak so esoterically that they prevent such a union, and yet it is perhaps they alone who have unearthed discoveries significant enough to revive philosophy's metaphysical life. Existentialism is, in contrast to Hegel's philosophy, in immediate contact with the everyday psychological and emotional existence of common men; so that, if it could provide a firm epistemological basis for a new metaphysics, it might convince even empirical philosophers of its validity. If such a new psychological foundation for metaphysics can be uncovered, it might go on to provide the greatest reversal of philosophical interests since Kant's Copernican revolution and make a fruitful relationship possible once again between systematic (i.e., metaphysical) philosophy and theology. Philosophy found its Copernicus in Kant; to find its Einstein among the existentialists would indeed be both strange and wonderful. For the future health and vitality of both philosophy and religion through their relation in metaphysics and theology, such a possibility ought not to go unexplored.

The Development of New Concepts

Assuming the principle that philosophy advances when new wine is poured into old wineskins, until the old containers burst and the contents pour forth in new forms, it might seem fruitful to place existentialist concepts inside a Kantian framework. Existentialism is responsible for the most radical ideas in recent literature and philosophy, and Kant produced the most rigid structure of the traditional views still widely influential. In the *Prolegomena to Any Future Metaphysics* Kant laid down the conditions which he thought must be met before metaphysics could again become a respectable part of philosophy. These prescriptions have resulted in the death of metaphysics many times over; and, although Kant foresaw that metaphysical questions would still arise to plague us constantly, most philosophers agree that the metaphysics which Kant himself envisaged as the aim of his own *Prolegomena* has never satisfactorily been written.

Kant set down the conditions for a rebirth of metaphysics without actually beginning the construction itself. At the end of his brief treatise metaphysics remained an actual, but not an authentic, science; it existed only as "a natural disposition of reason." [2] By his admission, Kant's own constructive attempt failed, at least in its first conception. This left us with only the critical framework upon which some future effort might possibly build, but no basis seemed available—that is, until the appearance of the existential psychological analysis and literary form.

Most of those whom we count as existentialists have not made any direct claim to be writing a new Kantian prolegomena to a future metaphysics, but, if their diffuse and often esoteric psychological jargon is placed within the more systematic Kantian mold, perhaps a completed *Prolegomena* will prove to be what in fact they either already have produced or may produce. The aim of the first part of this brief essay is to present the *Prolegomena* in a modern dress as a now completed essay in metaphysical psychology.

The thesis of this revised and contemporary *Prolegomena* is, first, that the revival of both constructive metaphysics and metaphysical theology depends upon the establishment of philosophical psychology as a legitimate enterprise and, second, that the existentialists have actually accomplished this task. Thus, metaphysics has once again been provided, by the existentialist analysis of what are essentially psychological terms, with the empirical material upon which it can safely build. This is exactly the empirical content which Kant found missing in his own day, the absence of which rendered "rational psychology" groundless in the eyes of the Kantian critique. The question now is this: Has the empirical content for the *Prolegomena,* which Kant himself was unable to provide, now appeared within the vast existentialist literature?

These Prolegomena are for the use, not of those who desire a completed system at one stroke, but merely for those who wish to make metaphysical questions meaningful once again.[3] There are technical philosophers who are interested primarily in the structure of language, and they naturally take what has been written down in books to be philosophy itself. Because of this orientation, they may not understand what existentialism can mean to philosophy, or how it has actually revived metaphysics through its psychological explorations and its literary effort. Before they can philosophize, such men must wait until something has been written down. Tracing all philosophy to a common origin in linguistic structure, for them all questions are to be treated alike. They often do not see that the source of all philosophical life is present in the psychological struggles which are familiar to every existing individual, and that it is this mundane source to which we must turn before we write or analyze the already written word.

Since everything that human reason writes down on paper is bound to have a similar appearance, owing to the transforming power which the written word exercises on all creative thought, it is not surprising that the resulting uniformity found in the printed history of philosophy should confuse some people into mistaking that finished product for the philosophical life itself. If it is to renew its life, philosophy must once again inquire into its origins and avoid an excessive concentration upon its already completed and printed product.

The Sources of Metaphysics

My purpose here is to persuade all those who think that metaphysics is impossible in its classical form that it is necessary to pause first to propose the preliminary question "What must

3 The reader may find it interesting at this point to note the parallels to Kant's original *Prolegomena,* since the material here, as well as in chapters 2 and 3, was suggested by a much revised "translation" of Kant's important work.

man be in his inner or in his psychological existence in order that through him metaphysical questions have come, and continue to come, into the world?" [4] Can introspective psychological explorations provide an empirical ground for metaphysical speculation? For if metaphysical questions spring immediately from the nature of man, we might find there an empirical ground for this more abstract enterprise.

Even if it can no longer be a science, as it might have been before modern technology placed the physical sciences on a new footing, still, why is it that the metaphysical enterprise is so subject to uncertainty and to dispute? Considering man's inner nature and the origin of metaphysics within such a subjective psychological condition, can we explain why metaphysics is bound to keep the human mind in suspense with hopes never ceasing, yet never fulfilled? We may, of course, end only by demonstrating our knowledge or our ignorance in this field, but it is possible that we might also find a new footing for metaphysics other than the scientific. Can we explain why, because of its origin in the immediate life of an existing individual, metaphysics moves constantly around the same spot, while in contrast every genuine science is continually advancing in a cumulative manner? To do so might be to find that metaphysics as a discipline is essentially distinct from the physical sciences.

Philosophers of science often shun the field of metaphysics because its standards for knowledge do not seem precisely enough defined to be capable of verification. If the criteria for evaluating metaphysics cannot be derived from the model of the natural sciences, then it is to the inner life of the individual, to him who continually gives metaphysics its birth, that we might try to look for our standards. Perhaps in him we may find an answer to give those who shun metaphysics because it does not arrive at precise conclusions, that is, if we can discover why the psychological origin of metaphysics necessarily makes its questions incapable of final resolution.

After all, it is not so extraordinary, considering that men became convinced that metaphysics was incapable of scientific

4 Cf. Sartre, *Being and Nothingness* (New York: Philosophical Library, 1936) , p. 84.

treatment, that the question should eventually occur to some how it had ever been possible to ask metaphysical questions about being and nonbeing at all. Common sense may delight in pointing out the puzzles to which metaphysics often leads, but sometimes this same human instinct can push aside elaborate arguments in order to propose the more subtle inquiry of asking how man ever came to ask such ultimately unanswerable questions about his own being in the first place? The inquiry into the origin of metaphysics in the private life of the individual is more difficult than the elaboration of logical systems, but it is never too late to become humane and wise. The question what in the life of every existing individual might give rise to metaphysics does presuppose a doubt about the possibility of ever giving finished answers to metaphysical questions, because it evidences an acquired sensitivity to the uncertainty which surrounds all human existence—and thus to all questions arising from that source too.

This lack of conclusiveness concerning the possibility of ever achieving certainty with respect to the fundamental questions evolved from man's individual existence will offend any whose whole view of philosophy rests upon a requirement of certainty. Those who demand precision in every step will take their internally rigorous systems in hand for comparison and look with contempt on anyone who suggests that the irreducibility of ambiguity and uncertainty can be traced to the psychological origin of metaphysics. Others, who seldom accept anything which does not correspond to some previous conception of what philosophy is, will not understand the consciously psychological and apparently personal language of the existentialist. Thus, what might have made possible an advance in metaphysics can in our own time go unnoticed because its suggestions are too radical to gain easy acceptance against some agreed definition of philosophy. Everything might remain for a time as though nothing had happened in philosophy to excite our concern or our hope for a revival of metaphysics and a change away from a philosophical analysis of trivialities.

Nevertheless, some readers, being already convinced that metaphysics is not a science, might still see that metaphysical questions can come to life again in another way; i.e., if the demands here stated can be satisfied—in other words, if an inquiry is made into the psychological possibility of asking metaphysical questions at all, so that the ground for the possibility of the question also gives validity to its answers, although no longer necessarily. This the existentialists have done, by explaining what it is in the psychological experience of man that gives rise to and empirical ground for such basic questions. There is as yet no such thing as a modern metaphysics in any completed comprehensive form, but the inquiry into its psychological origins may provide the necessary empirical grounding for its development. This will not take the form of a science, but it will be a series of crucial questions that arise out of the very uncertainty which any man encounters daily as he lives and moves in this world.

Metaphysics of this kind could be in great demand, even when abstract metaphysics might be temporarily out of vogue, since the ethical concerns of the common man are so intimately interwoven with it. Men must live and decide. If the existentialist can show us that one source of metaphysics actually comes from the interior experience of decision, a radical reform (or rather a new birth in a dramatically different form of procedure) is unavoidable, even if the traditionalists in metaphysics, and the anti-metaphysicians, may both struggle against it for a while.

A New Psychology

Since the psychological analyses made by Kierkegaard, Sartre *et al.*, or rather, since the modern rebirth of metaphysics as far as we can trace the history of existentialism, no application of this material has ever actually been made to Kant's own *Prolegomena* or to the later attacks on metaphysics by the Positivists and Logical Empiricists. Although the existentialists themselves have not replied directly and sometimes have said little about traditional metaphysics, they certainly have struck off a spark which may yet kindle a rebirth of that inquiry. Such metaphysical investigation is based on a new psychological analysis of the internal experience of a man, one in which he finds himself essentially alone in the world but still forced to act and to make ethical decisions. This psychological element of immediacy can give a new metaphysics its required empirical ground.

The existentialists often focus chiefly on a single but important concept in metaphysics, namely, that of man's direct knowledge of nonbeing through his experience of the 'dread' and the 'despair' which usually accompanies its presence. They have challenged reason, much as Hume did by his analysis of sense experience, to show that the questions of being and nonbeing arise from an immediate—i.e., from a personal and even an internal—experience (e.g., the permanent possibility of a negative reply to every question) and not from abstract thought, as with Descartes. Existentialism has challenged reason in order to prove that abstract thought actually cannot cope with the subjective problems of existence which men face as individuals when they are isolated and yet forced to make decisions in the midst of the human world. Existential analysis has given almost irrefutable evidence that it is nearly impossible for reason to understand the importance of contingency and uncertainty in an abstract way. Therefore, a new metaphysics which disclaims certainty might rightly be based on the psychological immediacy of experienced uncertainty.

Reason traditionally has sought necessity, but existence gives us only precariousness. In an abstract approach, philosophy might not see how 'dread' and 'anxiety' are pertinent to metaphysics, or how such concepts can ever be introduced into philosophy meaningfully. Hence many have inferred that metaphysics must be pursued scientifically or not at all. Others believe that those philosophers are mistaken who include existentialism within the province of contemporary philosophy, since such psychological and personal insights are nothing more than the concepts of emotion and thus are worthless for philosophical use.

Philosophers of a rationalistic persuasion thought that the existentialist analysis of the human struggle, couched as it is in immediate psychological terms, was nothing more than subjective feeling mistaken for philosophical insight. As such it could not serve as a basis for philosophy, at least according to traditional standards. Hence critiques of metaphysics have often implied that the human mind has no power to think decisively about such abstract problems as being and nonbeing. Existentialism did not relieve this judgment, because its concepts seemed purely fictitious and all its pretended profundity merely common experience falsely labeled philosophy. In plain language, since the old speculative approach to metaphysics was discredited and no one was able to exhibit the empirical relevance of the psychological categories of existentialism, many decided that there could be no such thing as metaphysics at all; i.e., one empirically grounded and yet at the same time abstract.

However hasty and mistaken such criticism of existentialism may be, at least in some instances such critiques rest upon careful attention to precision and clarity, and such methods of analysis have attracted many of the brighter minds of the day. Certain methods of logical analysis have been proposed in an attempt to raise philosophy above the level of dispute; and these methods, if widely adopted, would speedily result in a complete reform of the interests of philosophy. But the existentialist has suffered the metaphysician's usual misfortune of not being able to make himself understood. It is painful to see how many critics of existentialism, both sympathetic and unsympathetic, still miss the point actually raised by such a psychological analysis. The valuable suggestions of existentialism have often been misconstrued, and thus metaphysics remains in its old condition, as though the existentialists had not provided such problems with new life. The question is not whether existentialist terms are emotional and psychological or even inherently vague; this the existentialist knows to be inevitable due to the subject with which he deals. Rather, the question is whether the descriptions of 'dread,' 'meaninglessness,' and 'negativity' can provide solid and immediate data, a source sufficient to make metaphysical questions concrete. If this happens, it will be because these questions are now seen as an explanation of the most basic of experiences: that which makes man ask questions about the meaning and structure of his own existence. It is that experience which both produces and supports metaphysical inquiry.

If this new foundation for metaphysics is in any way correct, it would have an inner truth, i.e., one not independent of all common experience or restricted to an individual's subjective life, but a validity grounded in the elementary moral decisions which every man must face. This is the existentialist's problem: to add psychological depth to abstract inquiry. The present investigation concerns solely the origin of metaphysical questions in man's private life, a revealing inquiry which the ancients never raised exactly in this form. The issue does not concern the clarity, usefulness, or testability of metaphysical concepts. If we can decide what it is about man's inner experience of being-in-the-world that gives rise to metaphysical questions in the first place, questions concerning the validity, meaning, and application of metaphysics might be vindicated as a matter of course; i.e., by showing their ground in a basic inner experience of man.

The opponents of so influential a movement as existentialism should first of all begin their critique by penetrating very deeply into the nature of man as a living and deciding being, so far as such a form of psychology is relevant to philosophy. The allusive nature of this problem does not, however, suit a rigorous method of neutral observation. Some critiques find a more convenient method in being precise without insight, namely, in appealing to clear, distinct, and scientific modes of thought. It is indeed a great gift to possess precise, analytical methods and good technical ability, but such rigid procedures must somehow stop to take into account the internal facts of human existence which we all experience. A special kind of technical clarity cannot be appealed to as an oracle when no exclusive justification can be found for the particular way in which one has been trained to go about philosophy. Our inquiry will search out the ground for a possible new mode of philosophy, beginning with metaphysics.

A keen awareness of the sometimes desperate condition of human existence should restrain analytical common sense from claiming all of philosophy for its own particular methodology and approach. Thus, a rigorous logic and a speculative grasp of human psychology are both serviceable, but each in its own way: the former in judgments which apply to technical and objective observation; the latter in generalizations that are valid for every human being who understands what it means to live and to decide alone although still in the midst of a human community. This is the realm of metaphysics: the study of the basic structures of Being which determine both human existence and its experience of such essential isolation. Here, what calls itself, despite the inappropriateness of the adjectives, analytical and empirical has no exclusive authority to judge for all possible forms of philosophy.

A serious study of Kierkegaard is likely to awaken one from dogmatic slumbers and also to give investigations in speculative philosophy quite a new direction. Not that anyone is likely to agree in every detail with Kierkegaard, an impossible feat because Kierkegaard deliberately never arrives at any single conclusion. His work must be taken as a whole for its effect; any part taken by itself can appear trivial and may give no information to the casual reader. Let us start from the psychologically well-founded, but systematically undeveloped, thought which Kierkegaard (or the existentialists as a group) has bequeathed to us. Starting there we may well hope to do more to reconstruct metaphysics than that acute man himself did. To Kierkegaard we owe the first spark of this psychological insight into a side of man so often neglected by philosophy, i.e., dread and despair. Beginning here, all philosophy takes on a new orientation, since the starting point and crucial problem is usually definitive of any philosophy's form.

Systematizing a New Psychology

Following this suggestion, I first tried to see whether existentialist psychology could not be put into some systematic form. Soon I found that the concept of 'despair' was not the only psychological concept by which we could gain valid material for metaphysics, but rather that each metaphysical concept of importance can be traced to a genuine and significant psychological experience within any man (e.g., negativity, self-deception, absurdity). This refers to man insofar as he is internally free to determine his own fate, since the act of decision is what characterizes man in this analysis. The number of such concepts is as various as man's experience of himself, but all may be traced to a single starting point: man's experience of his essential inner loneliness in the world, coupled with the demand which society places upon him to make decisions.

I soon discovered that such principles are not merely of psychological and autobiographical significance, as the opponents of existentialism often try to say, but that they spring from the simple attempt of an individual mind to understand the meaning of its own existence; i.e., to form a psychological metaphysics. Such a simple and rational attempt to meet the problems of human existence is the fountainhead of all metaphysics and the only possible source for its justification.

Others have used similar psychological concepts, it is true, but only the existentialists have attempted to trace the origin of the feeling of, for example, 'negativity,' since few have had the acuteness to see the possible profundity that lies beneath human emotion. Spinoza deals with emotion, but as something which reason can eliminate. An investigation of the metaphysical significance of 'dread' and of the other existential concepts is the most difficult task which can be undertaken in the service of metaphysics. Unfortunately, present-day metaphysics cannot itself assist in this investigation, so little has the ancient discipline been learned recently, and so different is the usual conception of metaphysics from this psychologically based inquiry.

Only a derivation of metaphysical concepts from immediate psychological experience seems likely to render metaphysics once again empirically possible. Yet, as soon as one sees how vast the areas are which recent empirically minded philosophy has neglected, he may proceed safely, though slowly, to determine the whole extent of our immediate acquaintance with the source of metaphysics, defining the scope of metaphysics from its origin in inner psychological experience. This is essential if metaphysics is to be founded on a basis meaningful to every man—meaningful because he, too, is one who becomes aware of the precariousness of his own existence and then forms this experience into metaphysical concepts.

Nevertheless, the execution of such a plan to reorient metaphysics may fare no better than the original writings of the existentialists, which often have wide popular appeal but little technical use. It may be misjudged because it will be misunderstood, and misunderstood because there is something essentially painful involved in much of the existentialist analysis of psychological uncertainty. Trying to make sense of the mass of existentialist material is a disagreeable task, because the terms are often emotionally charged, obscure, and opposed to all ordinary notions of philosophy; and their analysis is often needlessly long. Still, it is surprising to hear such complaints, since the reward of a systematic understanding of the psychological basis of existentialism is nothing less than a new empirical grounding for metaphysics and a reorientation of the whole enterprise of philosophy. Their current popularity has sometimes been held against the existentialists, but this merely indicates how close they are to what is meaningful to those as yet unspoiled by technical philosophy in its logical and rationalist form.

As all existentialists admit, there is a certain necessary obscurity in their work, partly owing to the newness both of their terminology and of their whole endeavor, partly to the apparent lack of systematic structure in their views. But sometimes structure can be discerned only *after* the novel investigation has first been tried; existential insight is always retrospective understanding. In the process of any new investigation, it is possible to lose sight of the principal objective or, in pioneering, not even to be aware of it. This new Prolegomena is intended to remove the obscurity which sometimes surrounds the existentialists' aim by considering it in retrospect, as it is now possible to do. The whole of the existentialist writing, from Kierkegaard to Camus, will serve as the foundation to which these Prolegomena refer. We must have adequate and comprehensive empirical (i.e., literary and psychological) data before we can attempt to draw metaphysical conclusions afresh, that is, if we have even the most distant hope of gaining technical recognition for it.

Philosophers today are accustomed to seeing old knowledge presented as if it were new by means of a technically elaborate analysis. Most readers expect nothing really novel from existentialism; but this new Prolegomena may possibly persuade some that there is a new basis for metaphysics here, one which few—least of all the existentialists themselves—have yet explored in a systematic fashion, although a start has been made by

Heidegger and the phenomenologists. The very idea of using psychological and literary concepts in order to ground metaphysics empirically is a novel thought, and nothing before existentialism had made anything like this possible, except perhaps the internal reorientation introduced by Kant. Yet even Kant did not suspect that concepts derived from personal psychology for literary material could ever provide a systematic basis for metaphysics. Kant himself, despite his interest, ended in skepticism regarding the empirical content of metaphysics and left metaphysics aloft without an immediate grounding in experience. The perhaps unintentional result of the existentialist writing is to provide an empirical content for metaphysics, which, since it is drawn from man's most profound experience of himself, can give metaphysics both new material and a fresh orientation.

The door opened, even if unintentionally, by the existentialist to give ontological significance to psychological description and to literary form has never been suggested in just this way in the history of philosophy. In appraising existentialism, therefore, most men judge it according to the canons which are current in philosophy. Yet these canons are precisely what the existentialists mean to challenge. Adhering to such provincial ways, we are bound to see in existentialism only that which is similar to what is already known, because some expressions do sound familiar. Yet everything will be transformed away from the main existentialist intent, if one has in mind in advance his own conception of philosophy and does not really make an effort to grasp the new categories which they are trying to develop. The apparent repetition and lack of system in most existentialist writing and its unavoidable literary and dramatic tone are qualities which are essential to its point, even though they often make reading and comprehension difficult.

Few writers are gifted with the elaborate dialectical skill of Hegel or the intricacies of the thought of Kant. Still, the existentialists might have written out a more obvious and systematic treatment of their problems, if their object had been to contribute one more technical piece to the existing philosophical discussion. Instead, they proposed to challenge the very concept of philosophy and its current methods of procedure, calling philosophy back to examine its origins, all with the ultimate welfare and rejuvenation of philosophy in mind. In the long run their assault tactics may prove more effective than if they had sought to win favor by speaking in some current idioms or by conforming to conventional modes of expression.

The Reform of Philosophy

It is true that the existentialists have proposed a program of reformation that is much more opulent than they have yet been able to fulfill. Often they merely assail or ignore what they cannot meet directly. Yet more should come from the work of existentialism than its current popular shock wave, if its premises are sound and its psychological discoveries profound. Metaphysical questions, as they arise in man's encounter with himself in his own inner life, are such central issues for philosophy that, if the existentialist discoveries here are correct, all philosophy will be affected—if not in its practice, at least in its significance.

Metaphysics, defined as the investigation of first principles, cannot be corrected by anything other than itself, so that what we decide about the existentialist revival of metaphysics will probably determine how we approach every other branch of philosophy too. Whether existentialists intended this result, or were even conscious of it, existentialism will stand or fall on its claim to a revival of metaphysics grounded in immediate, concrete, and individual experience. But these claims which we make in the name of existentialism cannot really be accepted until the actual reconstruction of a systematic metaphysics is at least begun. To the present, all we have from existentialism are fragmentary bits of psychological analysis or attacks upon previous philosophy. In metaphysics there is either advance to an adequate and new systematic foundation for philosophy or there is nothing. The existentialists have thus far only proposed the revolution, and a few have begun the exploration (e.g., Heidegger); they have not delivered the fully reconstructed product. What the existentialists may not directly have intended for themselves we now propose to accomplish for them, in order that what they did discover is not lost.

This contemporary Prolegomena offers a sketch based upon the existentialist method and materials. What then remains is to complete a systematic revision of all metaphysical questions following existentialist lines. Only then can existentialism be seen as a structure capable of sustaining all of philosophy in a reborn life, a view which it had of itself, but which ironically it did not necessarily see coming via metaphysics. If the résumé of the existentialist method offered in the following Prolegomena still seems obscure despite all that has been said, it should be remembered that not all philosophers are bound to be metaphysicians. Many minds will succeed very well in the exactness of mathematical logic or in the intricate sciences which are more closely allied to the empirical world, even if they cannot deal successfully with metaphysics in its more psychological dress. In such instances, men are perfectly free to apply their talents to other areas of philosophy. But he who undertakes to make any pronouncements whatsoever concerning metaphysics or, more important, he who enters into a prolonged study of metaphysics can no longer overlook the proposals of the existentialists and their successors. Where metaphysics is concerned, no negative judgment or positive construction is now possible before one follows out the new approach of existentialism as it is now applied to metaphysics. If, understanding this proposal, he then chooses to reject it, he does so on rational grounds. To evade existentialism is no longer possible.

It should be remembered, therefore, that although obscurity is often abused and frequently conceals either indolence or dullness, still it has its uses as a defense against the untutored. Men who would disclaim knowledge in many areas of philosophy cannot be kept silent when metaphysics is mentioned, and it is not easy to expose their ignorance of the complicated documents in this field. It is useful to prove to some men that there are matters which are beyond ordinary understanding. Yet the often mentioned charge of emptiness which is made against metaphysics can be successfully contrasted with the concrete psychology of the inner life which existentialism offers as the heart of a new metaphysics.

If this new and concrete basis for metaphysics were to be accepted, all the hue and cry against the supposed tautological nature and the emptiness of metaphysical statements could be answered in the words of Virgil: "They defend the hives against drones, those indolent creatures" (*Georgics* 4. 168). The existentialists have, even if unintentionally, provided a new prolegomena to a contemporary metaphysics. Now, from this concrete literary and psychological material, a new empirically grounded metaphysics must be brought forth by their successors. It will be molded in a technical form perhaps not visualized by them but one nonetheless made possible by the existentialist revolt.

2

The Peculiarities of All Metaphysical Knowledge

Of the Sources of Metaphysics [1]

If we want to reconstitute metaphysics (and metaphysical theology) as a distinct discipline within philosophy, it is first necessary to determine accurately those features which make metaphysics unique. Otherwise we find that, with a revival of metaphysical interest (some aspects of which have already appeared on the contemporary scene), all parts of philosophy seem to become generally metaphysical. This only confuses the distinctness of the various parts of philosophy and makes it impossible to treat each part in the way that its unique questions demand.

When all parts of philosophy become metaphysical, there is no metaphysics and there are no distinct branches within philosophy for other specialists. Now, the parts of philosophy may be distinguished from each other by a simple difference of object, by the different sources of the knowledge which characterizes each field, or by the distinctive features of the kind of knowledge finally obtainable in response to the questions; or perhaps by all three of these conjointly. From such considerations, therefore, we should be able to determine the idea of metaphysics and its

1 The suggestion for the original structure of this chapter does come from Kant's *Prolegomena*, but it has been altered (as was intended) by the addition of new concepts and through the numerous revisions then required.

proper province within the field of philosophy and, at the same time, within theology.

If we first consider the sources of metaphysical knowledge, the very meaning of the term (i.e., that which is beyond or greater than a knowledge of physical processes) tells us that it cannot be derived directly from a study of any overt physical structure. Its principles and basic concepts can never be extracted from relations externally observed. It must not be external (physical) but internal (metaphysical) knowledge, namely, knowledge which has an inner origin beyond or behind external experience. It can, therefore, have for its source neither the external experience of objects as such, which is the source of epistemology proper, nor a priori knowledge, which is the basis of logic. Metaphysics is, then, based on an introspective psychology, one derived from the knowledge which man gains when he puts to himself questions about himself, particularly when he asks: How am I able to be; i.e., to ask questions at all?

But so far this would not distinguish metaphysics clearly enough from simple introspective psychology. Metaphysics must therefore be based upon *philosophical psychology* vs. *introspective psychology.* The distinction between these two attempts which man makes to understand himself is that introspective psychology simply attempts to describe and characterize man's interior states (e.g., phenomenologically), whereas philosophical psychology uses these descriptions of man's inner world merely as a basis upon which to reopen and reexamine traditional metaphysical and theological questions. Such philosophical psychology can be called *pure,* because it eliminates all reference to any particular individual. It treats psychological experiences and states as general conditions which are applicable to all men. Insight may be derived from this that will form a fresh approach to both abstract metaphysics and metaphysical theology. So much for the new sources of metaphysical knowledge, a topic to be explored further in chapter 5.

What Kind of Knowledge Alone
Can Be Called Metaphysical?

The distinction between analytical statements and synthetical insights

The special nature of its sources means that metaphysical knowledge consists of insights based on pure philosophical psychology. But whatever their origin or logical form, the content of the resulting statements divides them into two classes. The first are *analytical*, that is, explicative, adding nothing to the content of knowledge; the second are *synthetical*, that is, expansive, increasing the knowledge given beyond a simple description of the object.

Analytical statements tell us little more about the subject than we already know, although perhaps we do not know it quite so clearly or completely. When I say, "All men are aware that they are mortal," I have not really added any profundity to my knowledge of man; I have only analyzed it, since death was already known to be inevitably involved in the meaning of being human. To be a man means to be aware of one's mortality, though we do not always acknowledge this when we speak about man. This statement of philosophical psychology is therefore analytical. On the contrary, this statement, "The awareness of death may reveal to man the existence of nonbeing," [2] contains within it an insight which is not always actually thought of in the concepts of 'man' and 'mortality'. It amplifies my knowledge by adding something to my concept of man, something metaphysical (or theological) and not just psychological, and it therefore may properly be called a synthetical insight. The interior apprehension of death is the psychological counterpart of metaphysical nonbeing, and our emotional reaction to it not only reveals a metaphysical principle to us but gives us concrete material to guide its elaboration.

2 How 'nonbeing' can 'exist' and the metaphysical implications of this psychological discovery will be considered further in chapter 6.

The law of contradiction is the common principle of all analytical statements.

Since all analytic statements depend wholly on the laws of contradiction, they are in their nature a priori, although the concepts that supply their content may or may not be empirical. The predicate of an affirmative analytical statement (e.g., "All men are aware that they are mortal") is already contained in the concept of the subject ("all men"), and it cannot be denied of it without contradicting the concept. In the same way the negative form of such a positive statement is an analytical, although negative, statement mediated through the same law of contradiction. Such is the nature of the statements "All men are aware that they are mortal," and "No men are unaware (totally blind at all times) of the fact that they are mortal." For this reason all analytical statements are a priori in at least this sense, even when the concepts in the statement are empirical, as, for example, "Men are animals capable of abstract thought." In order to know this I need no experience other than my concept of men and of their ability to think abstractly. The whole statement is contained in the concept of man, and I need only analyze it without looking beyond it.

Synthetical statements require a different principle.

There is synthetical knowledge of empirical origin, and it is derived from an increased accumulation of sense impressions and succeeding experiences. But there is also another kind of knowledge which we perhaps learn only from the penetration forced on us by a single intense experience, and this comes from pure philosophical psychology. Statements based on both types of knowledge agree in this, that they cannot possibly have their origin simply in the principle of analysis alone, that is, by applying the law of contradiction. Although nothing can violate the law of contradiction, both types of synthetical statements require the addition of quite different principles to account for the knowledge produced, since the law of contradiction alone is not sufficient. First let us classify synthetical statements.

(1) Statements based on a particular experience are always synthetical.

Since the concept alone (e.g., man) is a sufficient basis for analytical statements, it would be absurd to try to base analytical statements on the testimony of individual experiences (e.g., "Each man in this group is painfully aware of being mortal"). That men are aware of being mortal is a statement which can be established from a single experience of a sufficiently penetrating quality, and it is not a statement based on extensive empirical accumulation. Even before we appeal to a series of experiences, we have all the evidence for the statement in a single forceful concept. From this concept we have only to draw out the rest of the statement according to the law of contradiction, and in doing this we become conscious that the statement is necessary; i.e., additional experiences could not be expected to add to it. All experiences are not on a par; all do not yield the same degree of insight. Some are revelatory; other experiences go no further than themselves.

(2) Philosophical statements based on psychological introspection are all synthetical.

This fact seems hitherto often to have escaped the observation of those who have analyzed human nature. In fact, it may seem directly opposed to all experimental psychological investigation, though it is both evident upon careful introspection and important in its consequences. Since most conclusions of contemporary psychologists are empirically derived (as all scientific procedure demands), modern men have persuaded themselves that all the fundamental principles of human nature are to be discovered by the same empirical-scientific method. This is a great mistake. A synthetical statement about human nature can indeed be established by empirical experiment, but only by adding to it as a context that fundamental condition of human nature into which all experimentation ultimately inquires. Empirical psychologists may discover something profound about the human situation but never simply from the procedures of empirical science alone. Such insight must be based on an astute grasp of their own inner experience as men, and here one intense experience is sometimes all that is required.

First of all, we note that most psychological statements of a revelatory quality are often derived from a single and disturbingly significant experience, rather than being accumulated by wide empirical experiment. This is true because any crucial experience carries with it an impact of depth penetration, one which never comes with quantitative experience alone. The abrupt, boundary situation limits us. It forces us to reflect upon ourselves, and this may reveal our structure as beings. This may not be conceded by the advocates of experimental psychology, but the analysis can equally well be exemplified in a more philosophical system of psychology (e.g., Freud's). The very conception of a psychological system implies that it will ultimately yield a general view. Theories do not originate in statistical experimentation, however much experiment may follow the original promulgation of a theory derived originally from a penetrating insight. To be systematic even in psychology requires theoretical structure, and theoretical novelty comes only from revelatory insight, perhaps itself the product of some single intense moment.

At first it might be thought that the proposition "man is mortal" contains nothing more than an analytical statement following from the terms 'man' and 'mortality' according to the rules of logic and language. But on closer examination, it will become clear that the real union of the two concepts often becomes clear only in a disturbing and personal experience, e.g., dread. In the midst of such an unsettling moment, the fact of our own mortality becomes clear to us without the mediation of logical rules. The realization of our own ultimate frailty by no means comes to us from mere thought about the relation between the terms 'man' and 'mortality'. Analyze these terms linguistically and logically though we may, we will not discover in these two concepts the psychological experience of the ultimate limitation of man with the same clarity that the feeling of dread can reveal this to us. We must go beyond conceptual analysis, calling to our aid some intimate and private experience which corresponds psychologically to the concepts of man and mortality, such as suffering through a seizure of despair, e.g., as Kierkegaard describes it in his *Sickness Unto Death*.

We must, then, work gradually toward a realization of man's nature, as it may be revealed in an experience of despair either concerning the self in general or death in particular. Hence our conception of our nature as men is really significantly enlarged by experiencing within ourselves one of the unsettling consequences contained in the proposition "man is mortal." We add to the first concept of man in general a realization of its meaning as revealed by the psychological impact of dread, and this is a clarification which no simple analysis of the term 'man' can produce. Some psychological statements are therefore synthetical, and they are the more plainly so the further we get from trivial experiment and mundane experience. For, in the major conceptions of man's nature, it is clear that, however closely the terms are analyzed, however elaborate an experiment is devised, we can never come to a realization of man's nature which is of philosophical import by a mere linguistic dissection of the term unless aided by the introspection of a revelatory but disturbing moment.

The same conditions hold true for any principle of psychology. That despair is inescapably a by-product of what it means to become aware of yourself and of your potentials as a self is a proposition that can become evident only in some moment of introspective insight. Empirically speaking and experimentally analyzed, my concept of 'self' contains within it nothing of despair as a necessary structure, but only as a quality occasionally experienced. The concept 'despair' is therefore altogether an addition to what external observation can reveal, and it cannot be obtained by an analysis of the concept 'empirical self'. Here, too, the intuition provided by a moment of disturbing insight must come to aid us. It alone makes possible the synthesis of despair as a necessary ingredient in the concept of selfhood. Penetrating insight, if induced by critical personal experience, acts as a synthesizing agent and makes philosophical insight possible. Thus philosophical psychology gains metaphysical import.

What usually makes us believe that the predicate (e.g., despair) of such statements might already be contained in the concept of self, and that the statement is therefore analytical, is the duplicity of our expression. We have a tendency to think of a certain predicate as attached to a given concept, in which case the concept cannot be other than as defined. But the question is not what in thought we somehow join to a given concept, but what we discover to be unavoidably connected through a depth analysis of the basic structure of the self. Without such moments of discovery, we cannot understand the self as it is related to despair, especially when the relationship remains somewhat obscure. Thus it may appear that the predicate (despair) belongs to this concept (self) necessarily indeed. Yet this is not discovered directly, but only indirectly, by means of certain extreme experiences which provide the intuition that must be present if we are to penetrate the surface. Individual 'moments' have philosophic profundity that general psychological experience somehow does not have.

Some other principles assumed by psychologists are indeed actually analytical and depend on the law of contradiction. Like propositions of identity, however, they serve only as a method for amassing material, not as fundamental principles of psychology. For example, man is gregarious, man has hidden aspects to his mind; or, men mature more slowly than animals. And yet even these, though recognized as valid from a mere analysis of terms or, more elaborately, through experimentation, are admitted in psychology only because they can be referred to some introspective but revealing moment of insight. The significance of any psychological concept is ultimately traceable to some personal and hence individual insight.

The essential and distinguishing feature of pure philosophical psychology, among all other philosophical knowledge, is that it cannot be derived merely from the analysis of ordinary terms or from accumulated experimentation but comes only from a reconstruction of crucial concepts. Therefore, in forming propositions we must proceed beyond the terms and find that which corresponds to the individual's interior knowledge of himself. Thus, such statements neither can, nor ought to, arise from either experiment or from the dissection of terms; they are, rather, all synthetically constructed out of prior internal experience; i.e., experience that results from certain unsettling situations, and out of the insights beyond the phenomenal appearance which such penetration yields. Meaning that is capable of sustaining metaphysics is uncovered only painfully and by the application of some internal force.

Both philosophy and theology have suffered some disadvantage from this neglect of philosophical psychology. Some modern psychologists have severed philosophy (an act they felt to be a service) from its most valuable province, namely, individual introspective psychology, since they felt it to be unworthy of either philosophy or empirical psychology. They take this enterprise to be dependent on totally different principles, namely, upon particular individual caprice alone. What they say amounts to this: that psychology contains only empirical, and metaphysics only speculative, statements. In this, however, they may be mistaken, and such a mistake has a decidedly injurious effect upon the whole of psychology, philosophy, and theology. If it were not for this, modern psychology (and philosophy) might have extended its investigations concerning the basis of our knowledge of human nature far beyond empirical experiment (and the analysis of terms) and could have included the possibility for a revealing if momentary subjective experience. Excluding introspective experience means the ultimate loss of depth of meaning and productive insight. Empirical investigation and abstract speculation have a meeting point and are unified in an intense experience internally apprehended.

Philosophers and psychologists ought not to base their rejection of metaphysics on merely empirical data and analysis without subjecting theoretical physics equally to a verification in experience, a process which physicists are too acute to allow. The new era of fruitfulness into which metaphysics and theology could have been brought by admitting the possible validity of internal insight would have saved it from the danger of contemptuous ill-treatment. Empirical objections would have to be applied to theoretical physics also, which would not be, and could not have been, accepted. Thus, men might have been led into psychological considerations similar to those which now occupy us, although this would have subtracted an air of rigor from their inimitably elegant style and precision.

(3) Basic metaphysical and theological statements are all synthetical.

We must distinguish statements which merely refer to metaphysics and theology from metaphysical and theological statements proper. Many of the former are neither analytical nor empirical; they only afford the psychological context in which to consider metaphysical statements. These actually are the whole aim of depth psychology and are always synthetical. If there are concepts admitted to be metaphysical (nonbeing, for example), statements arising from a simple analysis of them also pertain to metaphysics; for example, "Nonbeing is known empirically in the experience of dread." By means of internal pressure applied to several such psychological concepts, we seek to approach the definition of central metaphysical terms.

The analysis of the concept of philosophical psychology which pertains to metaphysics does not proceed in a manner different from the dissection of any other—even a scientific concept—not belonging to metaphysics (such as, "The experience of dread is accompanied by increased anxiety on the part of the patient"). From this it follows that the concept, though indeed not the analytical dissection of it, is properly metaphysical or theological. Analysis of statements is in itself a neutral act as far as metaphysics is concerned, and yet behind the statement may lie something entirely different. The discipline of metaphysics has something peculiar in its formation of statements from an introspective grasp, and this must therefore be distinguished from the features which it has in common with empirical psychology. Thus, the statement that "the experience of nonbeing is a permanent part of the being of a self" is a synthetical and properly metaphysical statement, although it is also possible to treat it in an ordinary analytical manner.

If the psychological concepts which constitute the materials and the tools of metaphysics have first been organized according to specific principles, their development can be of great value. Such use of individual psychological insight might be taught as a definitive aspect, one comprising nothing but that psychological analysis which is relevant to metaphysics, and it could be treated separately from the dialectical elaboration which constitutes metaphysics proper. For indeed, this particular class of psychological experience (e.g., absurdity or dread) is not of much value except to metaphysics. That is, this is true regarding the dialectical statements which can be generated by concentrating on certain crucial psychological experiences perhaps previously analyzed by psychologists. Metaphysicians may build on stones which the psychologists reject.

The conclusion drawn in this section is that metaphysics and metaphysical theology may be properly based on certain concepts drawn from philosophical psychology, and these alone constitute its empirical basis. To accomplish this certainly requires a vigorous dissection of its concepts followed by a dialectical elaboration, but here the procedure is not very different from that in approaching every other kind of knowledge in which we merely seek to render our concepts clear by analysis and explication. In this respect there is nothing special about metaphysics, and this methodological similarity has fooled some people into missing the peculiarities of metaphysical knowledge. But the generation of statements from the penetration gained from psychological insight constitutes the essential empirical basis for metaphysics and gives such knowledge its peculiar quality.

(4) The general division into metaphysical and purely psychological statements.

This division is indispensable, when a critical understanding of man's nature is in question, and thus it deserves to be recognized as a classical distinction for any critical understanding of man, although in other investigations it may be of little use. But this is the reason why dogmatic empiricists, who usually look for the source of metaphysics and metaphysical theology in pure reasoning instead of seeking their origin in philosophical psychology, have overlooked this psychologically important distinction. Thus, the celebrated Wittgenstein and his followers have sought to treat analytically statements about non-being as merely the products of a form of language, when it is clear that the justification and origin of such statements depend upon our ability to make metaphysical use of certain psychological experiences.

In Sartre's *Being and Nothingness,* however, there is an indication of this important division of statements. For in the early sections, once having discussed the origin of negative statements and their basis in our experience, Sartre goes on to indicate the fundamental character of the psychological experience of nonbeing. There is, however, no extension of this discovery to indicate its importance for making traditional metaphysical inquiry meaningful once more. Again, everything depends on our ability to isolate the psychological statements of potential metaphysical value.

So little has been done here to make this a systematic basis for metaphysics that it is no wonder that very few, sometimes not even the existentialists themselves, have been led to make an investigation into the possibility of a revival of classical metaphysical inquiry. The important consequences of existentialist psychology are not easily learned from reading their writings if you do not have metaphysics already clearly in mind. One must hit on this potential fruitfulness in one's own experience and reflect on the possible philosophical use of such existential psychology. Then one can find such metaphysical (and also theological) consequences everywhere, where one could not possibly have found them before. The existentialists themselves often did not recognize that such new principles were at the basis of their psychological sensitivity, which if recognized would make insight in other areas also possible once again. Men who never will think as radically as the original existentialists may nevertheless now have the acuteness to discover metaphysics' new basis, even though perhaps the earliest existentialists could not. Heidegger and others move toward metaphysics in ways which Kierkegaard, in his reaction to Hegel, could never have seen as possible.

The general question of the new prolegomena

How has metaphysics again been made possible? Were metaphysical analysis really alive and widespread, could we say: "Here is metaphysics; follow it and it will convince you irresistibly and irrevocably of its truth"? If this were so, the question of the basis for metaphysics would not be so pressing and there would remain only that other question: "How is such insight possible and how does human reason come to attain to it?" But human reason has not been so fortunate. There is no single contemporary book to which you can point, as physicists do to Einstein's unified field theory, and say: This is metaphysics;

here you may find an example of the noblest insights of this enterprise—e.g., the knowledge of being and nonbeing, proved from a demonstration of their possibility and explanatory fruitfulness. We can be shown many contemporary metaphysical and theological propositions; but these are all commentaries. They concern the materials and the scaffolding for metaphysics, rather than an extension of the knowledge of our basic nature and the meaning of existence, which is our proper aim in studying it.

Suppose you say, for example, "Nonbeing is integral to being." This statement has never been based, as it ought to be, on the philosophical use of psychological experience, even though its truth is conceded. You lapse, then, when attempting to employ such metaphysical statements, into such doubtful assertions that in all ages one metaphysic or theology has seemed to contradict another, either in its assertions or in its evidence. Thus, the demand for agreement has destroyed metaphysics' claim to be an enterprise basic to all of philosophy and theology. Even more drastic, many of the attempts at metaphysics were made without inquiry into its origin and hence are the main cause for the early appearance of skepticism in the philosophical novice. With this attitude philosophy has done such violence to its own value that it could never have arisen save from a complete despair over ever achieving philosophy's most important aspirations.

Long before the existentialists began to inquire methodically into introspective psychology, some philosophers consulted abstract reason for their metaphysics, which was of course to some extent still based on ordinary empirical perception, although the connection may not have been developed. This desire to reason abstractly is ever present, while a fundamental psychological base can usually be discovered only after great exertion and from the inner penetration which results. So metaphysics floated to the surface, like foam, which dissolved the moment it was scooped off. But immediately there appeared on the surface a new supply of dialectical fabrications to be ever eagerly gathered up by some. Others, instead of seeking the cause of the phenomenon in the depths of psychological experience, thought they showed their wisdom by ridiculing the idle labor of their metaphysical neighbors.

We have become, therefore, weary of the abstract dialectics of symbolic logic, intriguing and attractive as it is in itself but which teaches us nothing concrete, and also of an empirical skepticism, which does not promise us any insight regarding our own nature—even the quiet state of a contented ignorance. Disquieted by the importance of this basic self-knowledge which is so much needed, and made suspicious by long experience of all knowledge that is not concretely grounded, we ask the remaining critical question upon which the future procedure of philosophy and theology depends: "Is metaphysics possible on the psychological basis introduced by the existentialists?" But this question must be answered, not by the usual skeptical objections to the assertions of some classical system of metaphysics (for many never did assert that their statements had any basis in psychology) , but from the formulation, as yet only beginning, of a genuine philosophical psychology as a new metaphysical base.

In his writings Kierkegaard has actually treated this question synthetically by making explorations into depth psychology and into the conscious self itself. From this source he endeavors to determine the elements of the religious life and the ethical import of such discoveries. It is difficult to follow this sketch of his, partly because of Kierkegaard's perverse style. Thus, it requires a resolute reader, one who can penetrate by degrees into a psychological structure which is based on no data except the reader's own experience in following the author through his tortures. He rests his case as an author, and your agreement rests too, upon the inner reaction of the individual reader. Kierkegaard seeks, without external fact, to unfold self-knowledge from its original and internal basic insights. His reader may now carry this forward to draw a metaphysics from it, even if Kierkegaard did not himself envisage this.

These prolegomena, however, are designed for preparatory exercises. They are intended to point out what we have to do in order to make metaphysics actual, if it is to be made possible by the philosophical psychology of the existentialists. It does not aim to expound any particular new metaphysics yet, although a sketch will be started in part 2. This prolegomenon must therefore rest upon something already known as trustworthy, from which one can set out with confidence and descend to sources as yet too little known in the human self. Such discovery will not only explain to us personal experiences which we already were aware of, but it should also exhibit a range of insights that all spring from the same psychological sources. The method of prolegomena, especially of those designed as a preparation for future constructive metaphysics, consequently begins with introspective psychology.

But it happens, fortunately, that although from this alone we cannot yet assume metaphysics to be an actual discipline, we can say with confidence that our interior experience yields certain basic psychological insights. These in turn may be formed into a synthesizing force in philosophy, one which rests upon the philosophical psychology of the existentialists and that part of their literary movement which is of a philosophical nature. In both of these, certain experiences are unanimously recognized as being philosophically significant. Partly, this is on the basis of their similarity to all human experience, and partly it is by general consent that these particular experiences (e.g., meaninglessness, the experience of the absurd) are central to man's self-understanding. We have, therefore, at least some uncontested synthetical knowledge from psychology and literature and need not ask *whether* it is possible (for it is actual) but only *how* it is possible to transform it into a basis for metaphysics. Our task is to develop, from the principles which induce such experiences, the possibility of extending them systematically in order to construct a future metaphysics.

The general problem: How is it possible to derive metaphysical and theological knowledge from psychology?

We have already learned the significant distinction between metaphysical and certain kinds of psychological statements. The possibility of the simple analysis of metaphysical statements once they are made can easily be comprehended, since this is based entirely on the structure of language. The possibility of synthetical statements based on psychology, i.e., on those experiences empirically observed in ordinary situations, also requires no particular explanations, for experience is nothing but a continuous series of perceptions. There remain therefore only psychological experiences which are of sufficient depth and impact to be revelatory and thus useful for constructive metaphysics. This is the possibility which must be sought or investigated, because it depends upon principles in human nature other than ordinary sensory observation and surface reaction.

Here we do not so much need to establish the possibility of such statements as to ask how it is possible to make them, for there are enough of them which come from the existentialist writings to prove their existence. Since our present method is to inquire into origins, we shall start from the fact that such synthetic but psychological and yet metaphysical insight actually exists. But we must now inquire into the ground in man of this possibility and ask *how* such insight is made possible, in order that we may, from the principles discovered in its possibility, be enabled to determine the conditions for its use in constructive metaphysics, its sphere within philosophy, and its limits. The real problem upon which all depends, when expressed in a contemporary mode, is therefore: "How are psychological statements of metaphysical import possible?"

For the sake of popular understanding, the existentialists have often expressed this problem somewhat differently, as an inquiry into purely ethical or religious situations, and this they can do without examining the basis of the existentially illuminating insight. Since we are concerned here with metaphysics and its sources, the reader will keep in mind that when we speak of knowledge by psychology we do not mean an empirical analysis of ordinary perceptions but only acute situations capable of producing philosophical insight when apprehended immediately and introspectively.

The revival of metaphysics and theology in contemporary dress stands or falls with the solution to this problem; their future creative existence may depend upon it too. We cannot exist on past metaphysics alone, since those doctrines need continual renewal in order to produce insight. Let anyone make metaphysical assertions of whatever degree of plausibility (e.g., "Nonbeing must be conquered by the being of courage") ; [3] let

3 Cf. Paul Tillich, *The Courage To Be* (New Haven, Conn.: Yale University Press, 1952).

the existentialists overwhelm us with psychological and literary conclusions; but if they have not been able to answer this question satisfactorily, the positivists have a right to say: This is all in vain, baseless philosophy and false wisdom. The existentialists speak in psychological and literary metaphor and claim, as it were, to create metaphysical insights by dissecting extremely personal experiences. They assert connections which do not rest on any ordinary empirical psychology, and which they claim to have come to in privacy, quite independently of all external observation. How do they arrive at these metaphysical insights, and how can they justify such pretentious generalizations about man? An appeal to the consent of the common-sense meaning of language cannot be allowed, for that is a witness whose authority depends merely upon popular agreement. Says Horace: "To all that which thou provest to me thus, I refuse to give credence, and hate" (*Epistle* 2.3.188).

The answer to the question of the metaphysical validity of certain personal and crucial psychological experiences is as indispensable as it is difficult, although the principal reason that it was not sought long ago is that the possibility of the question could not have occurred to anybody in just this form before existentialism's vogue. There is, however, yet another reason: that a satisfactory answer to this one question requires a much more systematic, traditional, and historical reflection than the early existentialists were willing to take upon themselves, so much were they in revolt against tradition. The shock caused by the appearance of the first existentialist writing promised fame to its author, Kierkegaard, and this has reached its peak in our own time. But the extraction from the shocking material of its systematic-metaphysical possibilities has yet to be fully accomplished, although Heidegger, the phenomenologist, and others have each made a beginning.

Every reader who carefully reflects on what this problem requires must at first be struck with its difficulty, and he would regard it as insoluble and impossible if there did not actually exist psychological analysis within the existentialists' writings that is of obvious philosophical significance. This actually seems to have happened to Sartre (particularly in *Being and Nothingness*), although he did not conceive the question in its entire revolutionary quality as far as classical metaphysics is concerned; this must be done if the answer is to be decisive to a revival of metaphysics. For how is it possible, says Sartre, that when I make a negative statement I can go beyond it and derive from it an insight concerning the experience of nonbeing in such a manner that the latter is found to be necessary before negative statements can be possible at all? Nothing but existential experience can furnish us with such connections (Sartre concluded this from the analysis, which he took to be the end of the matter). That profundity, or, what is the same thing, insight into men's ethical and psychological structure, was for a time taken to be nothing but a phenomenon of ethical import and hence for merely personal and individual application.

Should my reader complain of the difficult and complex route followed by an existential analysis in attempting to work out a metaphysics, he is at liberty to solve the modern metaphysical dilemma himself in an easier way. If, however, he elects to probe the disturbing considerations involved in existentialism, he may after some trial feel surprise at the facility with which (considering the hiddenness of self-understanding) the question of metaphysics can be solved. Yet it has cost the existentialists years of work to furnish the psychological concepts required to give the analysis sufficient depth and bulk. Finally, we shall attempt the task of transforming their insights into systematic terms, not as a completed structure but as the necessary base upon which a new metaphysics can at least be suggested (see part 2).

All existentialist enthusiasts are therefore morally and legally suspended from their occupations till they shall have adequately answered the question, "How can pure philosophical psychology serve as a possible basis for metaphysics and theology?" We ought no longer to enjoy the reading of their literature and avoid the fundamental questions which are raised. For that answer contains the credentials which we must show when he have anything to offer to the philosophical world in the name of a psychologically based metaphysics. But if we do not possess these credentials, we can expect nothing else of reasonable people, who have been led astray so often by abstruse analysis, than to be dismissed without a real attempt at understanding. A rootless world is in need of metaphysical exploration, but a fundamental inquiry must be undertaken before the joy of building can begin.

If contemporary metaphysicians and theologians, on the other hand, desire to carry on their business (not as a discussion with a firm basis in human psychology, but as an art of wholesome persuasion which appeals to the fascination for the abstract, present in some men) this calling cannot in justice be denied them. Then they should speak with the modest language of those who indulge a pleasure. They should grant that they are not allowed to conjecture, far less to know, anything which is fundamental to the psychological life of man. Still, they do assume (not for practical use, which they must abandon, but only for the love of pure speculation) the existence of some psychological principles for self-understanding and the guidance of the will in its decisions.

In this manner alone can the dialectical (i.e., abstract) metaphysician be useful to philosophy and wise in his enterprise, and the more so as he renounces all concrete foundations for such metaphysics. For unless cautioned, we might assume that the latter could tell men something meaningful about the structure of our existence. When psychological life is under discussion, abstract dialectic cannot be the basis, for such speculation has admittedly ignored the question of its grounding in psychological experience. Merely abstract metaphysicians ought not to play with ethical advice, since the assertions made must establish their foundation in internal experience or else altogether ignore the attempt of unattached ideas to reach a practical connection.

It can be said that the entire philosophical psychology, which necessarily precedes all metaphysics and theology, is nothing but the complete exposition of the problem as stated here now gone about systematically and completely. We have previously had in various eras (e.g., Plotinus') a philosophical psychology. What has recently gone by that name is properly a part of either literature or empirical psychology. This present inquiry is intended only to constitute the possibility of the revival of metaphysical inquiry on the more immediate basis which ought to precede all modern speculation. And when a whole discipline is deprived of all help from other disciplines and consequently in itself is quite alone, as metaphysics at present is, it is not surprising that when we are required to answer a single question satisfactorily we should find the answer personally perplexing and troublesome. Shrouded in the celebrated obscurity of the existentialist writings, the "answer" for metaphysics is easy to overlook.

As we now proceed to this solution according to a contemporary metaphysical method in which we assume that such insights from human psychology actually exist, we need only appeal to two enterprises in human endeavor, namely, the psychological revelations of literature and the psychological analysis of ethical difficulties. These alone present sufficient material to us. Consequently if philosophical insight should be found in them, such situations can show the truth or the conformity of abstract dialectic to the human subject *en concrète,* that is, in his own experienced actual life. From this we may find a basis sufficient for proceeding to the ground of the possibility of metaphysics and metaphysical theology by an existential method. This facilitates our move greatly, for here abstract considerations are not only applied *to* facts but even are suggested *by* them, while in Hegelian metaphysical procedure they often appear to be derived *in abstracto* from dialectical operations. Existential concerns may now be joined with abstract elaboration to launch a new metaphysics on a new ground.

But in order to rise from these actual and well-grounded psychological materials to a possible knowledge of the kind we are seeking, namely, to metaphysics and theology as systematic and entirely creditable, we must understand what occasions all this effort. I mean the natural (though still suspect in spite of all its truth) apprehension of disturbing psychological factors which actually lie at the basis of metaphysical speculation, the exploration of which without any critical grasp of its full significance is commonly called existential psychology. In a word, we must comprehend the natural psychological conditions which precede such metaphysical inquiry. The problem may gradually be answered by a division into four questions:

1. How is it possible for certain psychological experiences to be fundamental to metaphysics and theology?

2. How is it possible for literature to be relevant to philosophy and theology?
3. How is it possible for metaphysics and theology to generalize from such material?
4. How is it possible for metaphysics and theology ever to become systematic and trustworthy?

It may be seen that the resolution of these questions, though chiefly designed to consider the essential material of existentialism, has something peculiar which deserves attention for itself alone. This is the search for the sources of any philosophical question in intimate psychological experience, so that the ability to consider abstract questions may be seen as of the inner self's own making and investigated and considered in this light. By this analysis these abstract enterprises gain, if not completely systematic conclusions, at least a basis for their legitimate use. While we throw light on the more profound question of the common origin of our speculative impulse, we might also explain more adequately the nature of metaphysics and theology as theoretical enterprises which are germinated psychologically.

3

Psychological Experience and Metaphysics

The Development of Psychology

Anyone who questions the enterprise here proposed may quite rightly have as his first question: How is it possible for certain psychological experiences to be fundamental to metaphysics and theology? And unless this crucial question can satisfactorily be answered, it will remain a stumbling block halting all systematic advance.

Psychology is a great and now-established branch of knowledge. Even though its separation from philosophy is recent, it encompasses much research and promises unlimited extension in the future. It carries with it now a greater degree of statistical precision and therefore no longer rests merely on a few observations. Consequently, it understands more about men than the mere sum of a limited number of experiments, and, moreover, it is thoroughly synthetical; i.e., it yields new knowledge.

Hence, the question arises: How is it possible for philosophy itself to obtain any psychological knowledge that is synthetic without psychology's experimental basis? Since the situation producing pure philosophical psychology neither is nor can be based upon ordinary overt experience, it must depend upon some more deeply hidden ground of knowledge. Such knowledge might reveal itself by its effects, if the signs of such crucial experiences could be diligently ferreted out. Only if philosophy proves to have access to revelatory experiences not open to experimental study can philosophy establish its own source of psychological insight and eventually ground metaphysics.

Psychological experience that induces philosophical discovery has this peculiarity: It becomes significant only at times of personal crisis, when human beings face their limits. Therefore, its most crucial insights are not derived from an accumulation of empirical experimentation. Its intuition is not strictly empirical, but pure, which means that its basic knowledge depends on a human insight gained at critical times rather than by simple accumulation. Without this, philosophical psychology could not advance metaphysics a single step; hence its insights always contain something of the intuitive. Philosophy proper, on the other hand, is more discursive. It may illustrate a doctrine through some intuition, but it never seems able to derive one from it.

This observation on the nature of philosophical psychology gives us a clue to the first condition of its possibility, which is that some penetrating and yet personal intuition must form its basis. Its concepts can thus be constructed and made concrete, even though not dependent upon, or even open to, direct experimentation. If we can uncover such personal insight and understand how it is possible, we may then explain easily how synthetical propositions are made possible for philosophical psychology, and consequently in what way such psychology can be fundamental to metaphysics and theology without being experimental. "Philosophical psychology" is an experience personally gained but of such depth that a universal condition is exposed, i.e., one capable of sustaining universalization.

For just as sense perception enables us without difficulty to enlarge our concept of an object by adding new predicates which sensation itself presents synthetically in experience, so, too, can introspective insight. In the latter, however, the synthetical product may be universally revealing and philosophically significant, while in the former it is only a posteriori and empirically cumulative. This is because additive sense experience or empirical experimentation contains only what is to be found in variable and contingent circumstances, whereas personal insight (if it is of sufficient force) is necessarily discovered in a crisis situation (e.g., the thought of life as absurd or the sudden realization of meaninglessness). Here, insight is of sufficient depth to be significant to philosophy and can be connected with the concept *independent of any individual experience or particular observation.* In the moment of crisis, all men are joined together, and the particular occasion itself seems unimportant. Oddly enough, such a unifying experience often comes precisely at a moment of intense isolation as the crisis "breakthrough" of such an experience.

But with this discovery our perplexity seems rather to increase than to lessen. For the question now is: "How is it possible to gain psychological insight merely from certain features of man's inner life?" Knowledge seems to depend on the immediate presence of a particular object. Hence it appears impossible to gain philosophical insight through psychological experience which is so subjective and momentary, because apprehension in that event would have to take place without any particular object as a stable reference, and in consequence it could not be publicly verifiable. Concepts are indeed such that we can easily form some of them a priori, namely, those which refer to very general and obvious human characteristics (e.g., man talks). With these no one requires that they be immediately related to a specific experience.

Take, for instance, the concepts of emotion and appetite. Even these require, in order to be meaningful and significant, a certain concrete use—that is, an application to some experience by which the object of such a state is present to us. But how can an understanding of any important human condition (e.g., death as representing the ultimate human limitation) ever precede the particular experience itself (i.e., dying)? How is it possible to understand my death before my particular time has come? And yet we do; and we even understand ourselves better precisely in such moments of insight.

If our psychological insights were of such a nature as always to represent things as they actually occur in everyday experience, there would not be anything which could really be called "insight," since understanding would in every case be quite specific and particular. "Insight" *connotes a direct and sudden grasp of some pervasive structure of human existence.* Ordinarily I can only know what is contained in any given individual experience itself, if external experience is really always and only what the mind deals with. If this is so, it is incomprehensible how any experience of a particular or special nature should make me understand anything about myself beyond the specific details of that experience, except as its consequences might become fully evident to me. Yet even this much expansion of the experience itself could not take place without additional insight of some kind, that is, without further reflection on the significance of the experience itself. Without this additional reflection, no ground for a relation between my particular experience and some generally valid insight could ever be imagined, unless the insight simply came without specific cause. In this instance its lack of connection would render it relatively useless.

Therefore, there seems to be only one way in which an individual observation can be a foundation for a significant insight and also be of philosophical import: *if my insight contains revelatory significance for some essential structure of Being, one brought to the mind's attention through a psychological experience of extraordinary penetration* (e.g., *dread*) . Such insight uncovers a first principle of my being, and of all Being insofar as man's condition reflects it. On such a principle much of Heidegger's analysis is built, although he does not extend it quite to metaphysics.

Nonbeing and the Analysis of Existence

That no man is capable of avoiding entirely the threat of nonbeing I can know from any single experience that happens to bring me unavoidably up against the limits of human existence. Hence it follows that propositions which concern the basic structure of existence are not only possible in philosophical psychology, but they can constitute a valid empirical base for metaphysics and theology just to the degree that they contain Being's first principles as experienced through a limiting situation. Also conversely, metaphysics on this basis can never concern problems other than those referable to or derivable from some fundamental condition of human existence, except as man's being finds its place in Being-in-general and throws light upon its structure.

Accordingly, it is primarily by psychological insight that we come to know anything about the general structures of existence. Only psychologically are we forced beneath the surface of experience, and that is where metaphysics lies. External experience, as Hume well demonstrated, is not such that it can disclose metaphysical principles. Psychological insight is that by which we come to understand the problem subjectively, i.e., in our own relationship to it as men. This does not require an objective uniformity of behavior but simply a universally applicable inner experience. And this assumption is necessary if psychological insight is to have philosophical validity or if, in case such insights actually occur, their possible revelatory power is to be extendable to metaphysics.

Now, at least two experiences are basic to all philosophical psychology and insure its metaphysical significance. These are *anxiety* and *dread*. 'Anxiety' derives primarily from a feeling of lack of ground; 'dread' is a more active state of being grasped by forces which oppose the structures of our being. Philosophical psychology must first show these experiences of stress to be basic to human nature, and then that such philosophical psychology itself is basic to metaphysics; that is, it must subject its insights to a depth analysis. If this is not done, it may be impossible to use them either philosophically or theologically. For philosophical psychology proceeds, not by adding together extraneous bits of psychological information, but synthetically—by an extended exploration of some single significant experience.

If depth is lacking in the experience, if it cannot support such extended exploration, there is nothing in it which can serve as the basis for philosophical analysis and synthesis. Clinical psychology is built upon an understanding of anxiety. Abnormal psychology would be without material if it were not for man's constant experience of dread, and the psychiatrist could not perform his art without some intimate awareness of the psychological burden which dread can create. Of course, these are practical applications, and what we seek is the *source* of the experiences; i.e., an origin which may be revelatory of Being itself.

If, however, we omit from the consideration of anxiety and dread all the practical manifestations which belong to professional treatment, still anxiety and dread remain basic human experiences, whether they produce clinical symptoms and are so treated or not. This means that they are experiences fundamental to man's nature as such, not just specialized or particularized in certain individuals who require treatment. Hence they can never be eliminated, although each individual patient may be relieved. But at the same time, by providing insights of philosophical significance (e.g., into Being and nonbeing) they prove that they must be fundamental to all human experience. They go beyond all empirical psychological study; that is, beyond a simple investigation of individual symptoms. In conjunction with such insights, it becomes possible to understand human nature in general, but only because they involve our own subjective relation to the fundamentals of existence too. In illness and abnormality, more that is fundamental to our being may be revealed than in good health, during which we simply go on accumulating impressions numerically until something brings normal life to a halt.

The problem of the present section has therefore arrived at one solution, at least. Philosophical psychology can be synthetical insights of a fundamental nature only by referring to no experiences other than those of a crucial and critical nature; i.e., when men are made dramatically aware of their irrevocable limits and of the precariousness of their stability. At the foundation of an insight so induced, there lies a primary grasp of anxiety and dread the significance of which can be found to depend on no single experience. The grasp of at least these two fundamental psychological aspects of existence is a general phenomenon experienced by all men to one degree or another and in one form or another. It is latently present before the understanding of any actual psychological experience, since in fact it makes possible the comprehension obtainable through certain particular moments which do not contain such general insight into existence within themselves. Yet this general ability to understand what causes basic uncertainty in human existence does not alter the peculiar circumstances of any actual experience of anxiety or dread which makes it empirically real. The only thing that is different is that anxiety and dread are grasped as fundamental to all of existence, and thus they open up our insight into Being on a new level.

Should anyone doubt that particular experiences can tell us so much about man's relation to existence in general, and not just about certain particular circumstances, we should ask: How is it possible to know how anxiety might affect any individual before we have studied the particular case history, or how can psychiatrists grasp the causes of symptoms *before* particular patients present them? Understanding a patient always requires that we go beyond the particulars of the symptoms presented. Such a penetration of barriers, however, is possible with anxiety and dread, and this is quite clear as soon as both are seen merely as general conditions which are disclosed in any situation of sufficient force to produce an understanding of that basic structure of existence. Then, the general comprehension of an individual problem, the final understanding of the conditions of any particular distress, can be shown to proceed from a moment of self-understanding; that is, from a subjective insight. What at first appears to be understanding of man only in his extreme phases gradually is shown to be a grasp of the center of his existence.

To add something by way of illustration and confirmation, we might simply watch the ordinary procedures of clinical psychology. All understanding of the individual patient's symptoms (when the clinician tries to match them up with classical patterns) rests upon this: that they may be made to fit a type, which is evidently nothing else than a mental synthesis resting upon the clinician's collected insight. And this insight must be basic—arrived at by subjective and inner penetration—or it would simply be as particular as that individual patient's experience and would have individual relevance only. In that case, it could only be said that what the psychologist found to be so was so and held good only for that individual case at that time.

That everywhere anxiety which cannot be attached to a specific object has at its base a fear of meaninglessness or the absurd (or both of them) and that anxiety cannot be accounted for alone by any specific set of objects or circumstances but only by the awareness of nonbeing—this is a proposition which cannot be supported simply from the consideration of the concepts. It rests immediately on subjective insight, and indeed on a significant and crucial insight, because it reveals something about the problems of existence in general. Upon such insight into the fundamentals of human existence the clinician's successful treatment of a patient ultimately must rest.

That we can know the effect of fear upon an individual, or that emotions may be classified into types and dealt with by Spinoza's method, presupposes a grasp of the significance of existence in general as it is revealed, say, by anxiety and dread. This can come only from insight, insofar as anxiety and dread are found to be dependent upon no specific objects, since simply from a series of particular situations no such general insight could be drawn. Consequently, the basis for philosophical psychology actually is some penetrating insight which makes synthetical and generalized propositions possible. Hence our metaphysical analysis of the importance of anxiety and dread to the revelation of Being explains at the same time the possibility of reaching psychological propositions with philosophical import. Without such an analysis—i.e., without the assumption "that everything which insight grasps as fundamental to existence, anxiety through insecurity and dread through fear, is grasped by us in its fundamental inner importance and not merely as external circumstance"—the truth of philosophical psychology might be granted, but its relation to metaphysics as its foundation could not be understood. Either subjective insight can grasp the basic structures of human existence or metaphysics is not possible on an empirical base.

Anxiety and Dread As Fundamental Structures

Those who cannot rid themselves of the notion that anxiety and dread are actually dependent upon certain qualities inherent in objects in the everyday world might exercise their acumen upon the following paradox. When they have attempted its solution in vain and are thus free from prejudice for a few moments, they might agree that the analysis could be well-founded: that anxiety and dread are dependent on no specific object and are able to be grasped and understood and dealt with only by subjective insight, not by or through any external circumstances or similarities.

If on two occasions the circumstances for producing anxiety are quite equal in all respects, it should follow that they can always be considered an identical anxiety and that the use of varieties of terms to describe the condition would not occasion the least perceptible difference. This in fact is true of various nomenclatures in psychology; but some anxieties exhibit, notwithstanding a complete internal agreement about their effect upon the individual, such a difference in their external circumstances that one case cannot possibly be put in place of the other. For instance, two anxieties based on a fear of death, one due to a mother's sudden passing and another said to be due to involvement in an accident, may be quite equal, both regarding their effect on the individuals and the proper method of treatment. Nothing is to be found in either patient's internal experience, if it is described as it affects his emotional state alone, that would not equally be applicable to both; and yet the one cannot be put in place of the other in its outer circumstances and causes. Here, there is no essential difference between the two anxieties; the differences which do exist our understanding cannot describe as internal, since the difference only manifests itself by external circumstances. But there are some examples from common life that are still more obvious, and all serve to show that two experienced states can be identical internally in their effect while being dissimilar externally.

What can be more similar in every respect than a boyhood dread experienced again by a man? And yet you cannot put the man in place of the boy now viewed in retrospect. For if one is a boyhood dread and the other is the dread experienced by a boy now grown, the one experience can never quite take the place of the other. In this instance there are no internal differences in psychological impact which our understanding can determine by inspection alone. Yet the differences are external, as insight tells us; for, notwithstanding their complete equality and similarity of impact, the man cannot become the boy again (time cannot be reversed). The experiences of one age never quite duplicate those of another, and yet we often say that the experienced dread is the same.

What is the solution? These two experiences of dread must not be determined simply by their particular circumstances, as some history might record them. They are merely occasioned by the circumstances. Both experiences of dread become the same because both penetrate the fundamental insecurity of man. The possibility of such insights rests upon the relation of certain things unknown in themselves (metaphysical principles) to something else (our moments of anxiety), and the experienced dread is often the moment in which this connection is revealed.

Anxiety is the manifestation of the internal penetration of insight into the possibility of nonbeing, and the external manifestations of anxiety can be explained only by connecting its external symptoms to the whole of experience of which it is a part. In other words, specific observable symptoms are explained only by their relation to specific circumstances; that is to say, the particular form which anxiety takes is explained only through a grasp of anxiety in its more pervasive setting. Less significant experiences are more directly connected with individual histori- cal facts, but it is likely that with more important insights the general grasp of the meaning of anxiety will become the focal point and the specific circumstances will fade. Hence the differences between the same anxiety experienced at two different times in life (for instance, the fear of death) cannot be made intelligible by any overt account of symptoms but only in relation to an insight which refers immediately to a subjective grasp that makes the general quality of existence plain and blocks out the specific circumstances at that moment. Circum- stances are forgotten as such, and what is remembered is the insight into the structure of existence.

Philosophical psychology, especially as it might have clinical implications, can have metaphysical validity only on the condition that it refers merely to such insight as that which reveals a general principle by means of, but without specific attention to, the symptoms and circumstances. But in regard to the general insight, the principle holds good that such insight is not into the external conditions but into the subjective effects of the particular anxiety; i.e., its penetration into the being of the patient. Hence it follows that the findings of philosophical psychology are not the result of a mere creation of our poetic imagination, and yet they cannot with assurance be referred to any specific external circumstances.

These findings become valid for all forms of anxiety, because generalized anxiety is not specifically the result of any given set of external conditions. It is an internal insight into the basis for all particular anxieties. Insight, the exploration of which is the basis for philosophical psychology, often results from the internal penetration of any psychological state, which a recitation of the external circumstances may induce but does not wholly explain. Therefore, these insights can never contain anything but what a basic grasp of human existence prescribes to them. Insight never comes from the external conditions and it cannot depend upon them. If it did, all physicians should have equal power—given an equal accounting of the circumstances—to heal the internal condition, which certainly is not true.

It would be quite otherwise if human existence were so constituted as to yield insights into our basic condition from merely external observation. For then it would follow from the appearance of an anxiety, which with all its symptoms serves the clinical psychologist as his material foundation, that this information would be sufficient to yield insight. Yet this is something which every man in trouble knows not to be true. The anxiety uncovered by the clinician would be considered merely related to that symptom and would not be credited with any ability to yield insight for all sufferers. We cannot see how a variety of particular human complaints can of itself form a class image, whereas we know that a general concept is often formed through the insight gained from a single symptom; all this precedes our acquaintance with the whole range of individual maladies.

This class image, or rather this formal classification, is the essential product of some unusual and special insight which alone causes a variety of symptoms to become meaningful to us. (The symptoms were well known long before Freud achieved his insight.) Such crucial insights represent, not a general and cumulative grasp of a mass of symptoms, but a subjective insight often resulting from a single penetrating experience. Now we can easily comprehend, and at the same time give evidence for, the fact that all internal penetration into our psychological life does in fact give order in the most precise way to the findings of clinical psychology as a collective body of information. This is due to the fact that such insight, by means of its form of internal penetration—e.g., via the analysis of the basis for anxiety with which the clinical psychologist is occupied—makes those symptoms explainable through a subjective penetration. A "break through" is an instant that grasps a principle of human existence and no longer a particular symptom.

The Universality of Psychology

It will always remain a remarkable phenomenon in the history of philosophy that there was a time when even psychologists who were at the same time philosophers began to doubt their ability to achieve metaphysical insight. Not that they doubted the accuracy of their clinical diagnoses so far as the theory concerned some particular anxiety, but that they doubted the applicability to all men in general of the insight which the appearance of anxiety, with all its accompaniments, gives us into the nature of our being and into Being in general. We have often shown much more concern over whether anxiety could be classified into four or five types, and consequently whether a particular symptom in an individual might exemplify several types; all the while the anxiety which the individual experienced did not seem to be relieved or explained by mere classification. Empirically minded psychologists cannot be expected to recognize that it is the presence of nonbeing in nature which renders all anxiety possible. That is, the apprehension of nonbeing as fundamental to all Being produces the individual experience. This basic anxiety is not to be understood merely by describing its details or classifying its types. It is an experience to be penetrated only by a subjective psychological insight of such extraordinary depth and force that the human condition itself is revealed. After all, as we have already said, the symptoms themselves had been known for centuries before Freud's insight drew its profound analysis. Something must come to force the mind beyond a series of symptoms or a recital of individual external conditions.

Any symptom of anxiety affords an opportunity for insight; that is, it may provide an occasion for internal psychological penetration. But in such a case, the particular anxiety uncovered by the clinician is exactly the same as that psychological state which serves as a basis for the philosophical use of psychology. Anxiety is the basis for the possibility of all internal insight and as such it is a clinical case situation not without philosophical import. Our basic psychological insight does in fact agree with the diagnosis of the clinician, which he may draw from analyzing any momentary symptom, whereas the metaphysician finds in this same situation the revelatory basis which can provide the internal penetration that yields insight into Being itself. In this way philosophical psychology can be secure in the undoubted applicability of its insight to all who suffer against all the diversions of a too shallow, statically minded psychology. Such empirically oriented psychology is often surprised at any metaphysical insight, because no one has yet traced these to their source in the internal understanding of man's psychological nature.

Whatever psychological symptoms are to become generally meaningful must be made so through philosophical insight. All our insights, however, take place by means of an understanding of human existence; discursive reason has no insights of its own here but only reflects upon this fundamental grasp once achieved. We have just shown that human existence never enables us to come to know things which are fundamental to our internal life either abstractly or merely from external observation. Since understanding comes only through insight, which is an evidence of subjective grasp, we conclude that "all symptoms, together with the particular anxieties which give rise to them, must be considered as nothing but occasions for the self's internal psychological penetration. Insight exists nowhere but in our subjective grasp of our own being as prompted by the external conditions." Is this manifest philosophical idealism? Not really.

Human beings and their symptoms are empirical entities; only Being, its basic structures, and the understanding of it are not.

Strict empiricism consists in the assertion that there is no means of apprehension except discursive reasoning about particular events. All other things which we think are grasped by insight are nothing but passing moods in the thinking being—internal penetration, perhaps, but not capable of being supported with facts. On the contrary, what we say here is that symptoms which are common in human existence become fully meaningful only through some internal penetration occurring during or after a moment of crisis or pressure. We learn nothing of them abstractly or casually. We know them only through subjective insight: through the changes which they cause in us by affecting our power to grasp human existence.

Consequently, we ought to recognize that there are powers deep within us which, though their meaning is quite unknown to us, we know to exist by changes which their influence produces on our powers of insight. These changed conditions we might call "states of suffering," a term signifying merely the insight afforded by a condition whose specific causes are still unknown to us but which are not therefore less real psychologically. Can this be simply termed "subjectivism"? In fact, it is the very contrary. These powers when touched within us produce concrete changes; *the state is perfectly objective but the insight is subjective.*

The Necessity of Subjective Insight

Long before Freud's time, and assuredly since then, it has generally been assumed and granted, without any detriment to the actual existence of empirical psychology, that many symptoms produced by our internal states may be understood only by subjective insight. They have no proper mode of apprehension outside our own internal grasp of the changes taking place, at least some of which are not always externally evident. Insecurity, inferiority, and loneliness, for instance, are of this kind. Now, if I go further and classify the remaining primary forms of suffering—such as fear, lack of confidence, and, in general, anxieties and their accompaniments (nervousness or unsteadiness, worry, etc.) —no one can in the least adduce the reason for their being considered avenues of insight. The man who finds that inferiority is not to be explained fully as a symptom of a quite particular circumstance and overt condition but is only to be understood as an internal psychological state should not on that account be called a "subjectivist." And this thesis should not be named subjective merely because it finds that *all the forms of suffering which produce overt symptoms depend for their understanding simply on a penetrating internal insight.* This is an objective condition subjectively understood.

The existence of an understanding based on insight is not destroyed by this analysis, as it is in a strict empiricism. We show, rather, that we cannot possibly learn the causes of anxiety from its external evidences, whether perceived in general or considered abstractly. What would our assertions here have to be to avoid all subjectivism? Undoubtedly, that the evidence for the causes of anxiety is contained in the overt manifestations of the symptom—and that I have not said. That the symptom can be understood through its overt manifestations is an assertion in which as little meaning can be found as in the statement that the symptoms of anxiety need only be recorded and not explained. The patient knows the external situation and the circumstances better than any doctor ever can, and he could cure himself were the causes to be found there. But it is for the depth of their subjective insight that doctors exist, and by it they are able to reach a cause beneath a surface which they can never fully exhaust in its detail.

Hence we may answer an easily foreseen objection: "that, by admitting the empirical inaccessibility of the basis for anxiety and dread, the whole scientific world would be turned into a mere sham." The philosophical analysis of the nature of psychological insight would be spoiled if it made such insight merely a confused mode of empirical evidence, according to which we know psychological states as they are but are not able to reduce everything in our evidence to a clear statement. I have explained above that insight consists, not in this logical distinction of clearness *vs.* obscurity, but in the genetic one which involves the origin of a knowledge of our inner life. For psychological insight grasps internal states, not at all as they appear on the surface, but only through the mode in which they affect human existence at its base.

Consequently, by psychological insight subjective situations are made available to discursive reason for reflection. After this necessary correction, an objection could arise only from a failure to see the separate and yet parallel relation between subjective insight and overt condition. This doctrine does not attempt to turn all the things of the empirical world into unimportance but, rather, to explain empirical symptoms through internal psychological penetration. Although the symptoms are there, the causes for psychological illness do not themselves lie in the empirical world. And in certain situations we receive the power to penetrate behind this.

When an insight comes to us we are still quite free in evaluating the matter. The occurrence of insight depends upon our internal sensitivity, but the value structures which we apply to it depend solely upon the values selected for emphasis. The only question of fact is whether or not, in the structure of that particular psychological state, there is some truth to be discovered, however it is to be evaluated. But the difference between truth and dreaming is not ascertained from the nature of the external evidence derived from observing psychological patterns. To ascertain the truth, we must connect various internal states; when the separately discerned parts are properly related, an insight results which could not be present in each part alone. We now determine whether this structure revealed in insight could be part of any or all of human existence. And it is not the fault of insight if our internal grasp should momentarily take illusion for truth. The insight, by which the psychological state of even an unstable person is made vivid to us, can be correct, but it is still a fact which discursive reason must analyze and test.

Human existence seems to show us that the course of man's life is progressive, not retrogressive. This may be true. If we mean nothing but a continued and cumulative subjective insight into our inner life, we do not decide about the objective character of any man's progress. But a false judgment may easily arise if the mind is not on guard against considering this revelatory mode of internal evidence objective. Men sometimes appear to move backward. It is not our insight into human existence, however, which must be charged with the illusion, but discursive reason, whose province alone it is to decide whether an objective conclusion can be formed from a subjective insight. We may increase our internal understanding and still regress objectively, and vice versa. Internal insight, valuable as it is, still requires objective evaluation. The two sides must keep each other in check.

If we reflect on the origin of our evidence whenever our insights into human existence concerning the inner life (e.g., anxiety and dread) are such that a source of our psychological life is made clear—when before it was not—illusion or truth will arise, depending upon whether we are negligent or careful. Insight does not dispense with caution. It is merely a question of the careful use of psychological insights in discursive reason; it is not an issue over the origin of insight or what it reveals. All uncertainty about human existence, together with its basis in anxiety and dread, is nothing but an *occasion* for some subjective insight. Anxiety and dread are merely the basis for insight which cannot be experienced by men not subject to their dreadful grasp, but these states are not the insight itself and alone cannot guarantee it. If I make use of the resulting insights for metaphysics, there is no reason for me to regard them as subjective insights that necessarily lead astray or cause illusion. For all the checking they require, they may still yield a base of metaphysical significance; they may still give us a truth about the internal life.

Any diagnosis of a particular patient by clinical psychology will, if carefully done, tell us something about anxiety as a general phenomenon as well as about the psychological states which are basic to human existence. Consequently, it can form a basis for all metaphysics. It is a foundation derived from the internal life, whether I consider anxiety merely the occasion for insight or something which is itself a part of the basic state of man and thus is involved in the insight itself. In the former consideration, however, I must discern how I can know from philosophical psychology what is basic to all the psychological states which are probed through such internal penetration. Otherwise, everything regarding a metaphysics or a theology based on the internal life would remain just as if we had not departed from the common empirical view.

Extending a Basis for Metaphysics

We should venture to go beyond a simple description of the interior life using merely the concepts of anxiety and dread. And we cannot refrain from doing this if we declare them to be symptoms of a basic human state upon which metaphysical concepts may be formed. For what should prevent us from applying them to all men, although each individual human existence may be quite different and even appear externally not to be involved with them? A grave error might arise, owing to an illusion, if we should proclaim such concepts to be externally and objectively applicable to the overt behavior patterns of all who exist. What seems merely a subjective condition which is productive of psychological insight is not therefore certain when applied to external behavior, because it is only an internally based metaphysics. I cannot extend this internal condition to a general description of overt behavior; I must limit it to a metaphysics based on a grasp of Being via the internal life.

The doctrine of insight produced from a subjective apprehension of anxiety and dread does not therefore reduce the whole of human existence to a uniform pattern. It is the only means of extending the application of one of the most important kinds of knowledge (that which a philosophical psychology teaches us is basic to existence) to internal human states and of preventing it from being regarded as mere illusion. Without this observation, it would be quite impossible to determine adequately whether the psychological insights afforded by anxiety and dread, which we borrow from no simple experience of the internal life and which are basic to the insights of philosophical psychology, are not mere phantasms of our brain to which only psychological states correspond. Consequently, our concern is to be able to show its unquestionable validity with regard to all the psychological states of the internal life. Although often derived from literary insights, this indicates our indirect relationship to all basic states of existence. We can discern the basic structures of Being only indirectly, never directly; thus the metaphysical relevance of psychology.

These principles do claim to form powerful insights out of the internal experience provided by human existence, but they are far from turning the truth of the external life into mere illusion. They are, rather, the only means of preventing the empirical illusion that our external modes of life define our existence, by which metaphysics has hitherto often been deceived and led to the childish endeavor of catching visible bubbles. Subjective insights, which are only signs, were taken to be individual and not extendable to general conditions. Here originated the remarkable occurrence of Kant's antinomy of reason—that inner states could never be made to conform to external observation. This antinomy can be solved by the single observation that penetrating insights, as long as they are employed in relation to the general condition of human existence, are able to produce truth. But the moment they transgress the bounds of the internal life and attempt empirical description (i.e., are applied externally and concretely without change), they produce nothing but illusion, since the true states never in fact correspond to the description exactly in every detail.

Therefore, I leave to the things we obtain by insight into human existence their actuality. By this theory we limit our psychological insight into these states only in this respect: that it represents nothing more, not even in the basic insight derived from anxiety and dread, than a penetrating insight into those states and in itself prescribes no particular pattern of external behavior. Since we never attempt to describe the external symptoms or the overt behavior that may or may not result, this is not a sweeping illusion invented for psychology by this analysis. My protestations, too, against all charges of pure subjectivism are valid if given a certain view of philosophy, but unfortunately the criteria in philosophy are not so certain. Some cannot see any doctrine except in terms of their own nomenclature. They cling only to a certain strict usage of terms and thereby deform and transform every new doctrine into a form of their own.

I would myself give this theory the name "existential empiricism," an empiricism of concrete inner states. The name should not lead anyone to confound it either with the rigid empiricism of Ayer (indeed, his was an insoluble problem, since he thought everyone at liberty to ignore the existence of the internal life because its insights could never be verified satisfactorily) or with the mystical and visionary idealism of Buber. Our critical treatment should contain the proper antidote, since it attempts to ask the crucial questions which must be asked if the validity of an internally based metaphysics is ever to be established.

This psychological (and thus existential) empiricism is not concerned with the existence of universal notions (the doubting of which, however, constitutes empiricism in the ordinary sense), since such notions do exist but may not be immediate or concrete enough to ground a metaphysics. Our concern is the psychological insights derived from the internal states that anxiety and dread particularly illustrate. Concerning anxiety and dread, and consequently all psychological states in general, I have hoped to establish their immediacy and their universal appearance internally, if not always externally, and thus to determine that the insights which they can produce at moments are of metaphysical value.

The word "existential" for me never means a reference to our knowledge of overt human behavior, with which the popular doctrine often confuses it, but rather it concerns only our own internal grasp of existence. Yet, rather than give further occasion to it by this word, it is equally possible for this empiricism to be called "critical." But if this is really an objectionable use of empiricism—i.e., to view actual psychological states as inducing subjective insights and as our only evidence from our inner life—by what name shall we call the converse changing of internal evidences or signs into overt psychological states? Such a view may, I think, be called "oversimplified empiricism," in contradistinction to the former, which may be called "critical," since it bases metaphysics on internal insight, but not without asking the critical questions first concerning the grounds for such metaphysical use.

If an inner state is never confused with any particular outer behavior, a constant state may be seen to be present beneath a variety of overt behavior. Insight into such a universal condition of existence can then be extended to ground metaphysics in experience—an inner experience and not necessarily a uniform outer experience, to be sure, but still an experience whose basis has been explored critically. The insight comes in a moment, psychologically and internally, but, when critically examined, it may prove to have universal adaptability. Overtly we often seem to be cut off from the rest of existence and from all Being, which limits the extension of metaphysical principles when they are established overtly. Internally, particularly in moments of crisis, we learn about our membership in the community of beings. Insights thus derived we are then able to extend unhesitatingly to Being in general, as long as we do not always insist that a uniform overt state must accompany a universal aspect of Being whenever it is internally experienced.[1]

1 The reader will easily understand that this investigation is a systematic inquiry into fundamental issues and not a comprehensive appraisal of all the literature already written along these lines. It is true that at times I seem to write as though I were the first to consider these matters, but that of course is merely a matter of style in developing the question. What I hope is that this investigation will bring the issues and the material together into a systematic inquiry that can again ground metaphysics. To try to write a survey of all the relevant literature would be a quite different undertaking. Nevertheless, the reader may wish to compare this attempt with Jose Farrater Mora's effort to produce a theory of being by combining existentialist and naturalistic reflections on death, in *Being and Death* (Berkeley and Los Angeles: University of California Press, 1965).

Hazel Barnes has done much to clarify the theoretical significance of Sartre's work (e.g., *The Literature of Possibility* [Lincoln, Nebr.: University of Nebraska Press, 1959]), although she has not quite used Sartre for the construction of technical metaphysics.

It is hoped that the use of 'insight' in this chapter has been clearly defined in the context of the argument, but the reader may wish to compare it with two other famous uses of that term. Cf. Bernard Lonergran, *Insight* (New York: Philosophical Library, 1957), and Michael Polany, *Personal Knowledge* (Chicago: University of Chicago Press, 1958).

The whole movement of "existential psychoanalysis," of course, has not quite taken the metaphysical direction of the present investigation, but it is certainly complementary to these questions and also provides supporting evidence. See, for instance, *Existence*, ed. R. May *et al.* (New York: Basic Books, 1958); Ludwig Binswanger, *Being-in-the-World* (New York: Basic Books, 1959); and Erwin Straus, *Phenomenological Psychology* (New York: Basic Books, 1966).

Allowing for a more phenomenological path, Merleau-Ponty has worked in this same direction. See Remiguis Kwant, *From Phenomenology to Metaphysics* (Pittsburgh: Duquesne University Press, 1966).

4

Metaphysics and the Life of Literature

The New Literary Approach

That the existentialist movement has developed as much within literature as within philosophy raises the following question: How is it possible for literature to be relevant to systematic construction in philosophy and in theology? Is this an accidental association, or is there some basis common to them which can be explored to reveal a systematic connection? Literature, particularly a novel or play, reveals the existence of human beings by opening to view the reaction which one human being has upon another, but it does this in a way not found in ordinary experience. If literature somehow had to reveal the existence of human beings exactly as we ourselves experience it, we could never know human nature any more clearly than in just the way we find it in our own day-to-day existence. We do not live in a world with *No Exit,* and yet we learn about ourselves when Sartre puts us in such a literary world.

How can we ever learn what belongs to human nature as its essential structure unless a way is found to disentangle the fundamentals and to lay them bare to our view? This a philosophical novel can do by extracting what is important and by leaving behind the obscuring detail. I do not want to know what is obtained by examining the detail of my own internal life, for that leads me only to an unfruitful self-definition of limited application. What I want to know are the fundamental structures of life's intercourse. We may find in significant literature some aspect of the self's essential structure revealed through examining the interactions which take place in a dramatic moment.

I learn the most from that situation in which a human being, otherwise in isolation, has his structure revealed through relationships that he enters into with concrete persons. These contacts develop forms of existence that draw him out of his isolation. Reflective thought, by which alone I can understand the structure of existence as it appears in human beings, requires that the inner life be drawn out and made overt in a way that ordinary experience does not reveal it. Other human beings do not always seem to conform to my own internal mode of life as I know it, but in human intercourse reflection is often able to grasp some essential of the inner life now made evident.

Thus I discover the essential kinship of man, but first this may have to be presented to me through literature. From its characters I may gradually discern a concrete picture of internal existence, placed in verbal, and to that extent visual, terms. Literature makes private life and thought public. I now live with Roquentin and, thanks to Sartre, experience *Nausea* with him even though it is not clear in my own experience. The inner life of man is rendered immediately overt in words in a way in which our own actions can never correspond to our inner disposition. If a novel or a play is successful, philosophically speaking, an instable inner life is transformed for public view and made stable through the power of words and the author's mastery over them. At the author's bidding words reveal and fix in our minds what otherwise would be only dimly seen and fleetingly grasped.

Literature's power of concrete characterization is important philosophically because human nature cannot be known simply externally. Rather, it is revealed only after its existence in a community has been defined. This comes about through specific situations which both structure and at the same time reveal the inner life. Now we join the besieged city and, through Camus' artistry, face the revealing power of *The Plague*. For a philosophy interested in the inner life, literature and drama can once again provide central and irreplaceable data. Yet knowledge of a human being, via literature, as he is in isolation is still equally impossible, since even inner existence can be made definite only by contact. If internal experience is to teach us the modes of activity to which human existence is subject, these modes should not have reference only to human beings in isolation, for they would not then be of philosophical significance.

Moral problems, then, are the root of our knowledge of existence, and they arise only as relations develop between individuals (even when, as with Job, the other person is God). Our own internal life teaches us, however, both that an inner life exists and how it exists, but never how it must necessarily exist in relation to others or that we and they must act so and not otherwise. Our own internal life, therefore, can never teach us about the nature of all human beings apart from our own intercourse with them. The mechanics of our external relations are of course easily observable; but literature portrays an inner life by clothing it in verbal and thus visual form.

We actually possess a body of literature of philosophical and theological import in which human modes of activity are laid bare and around which a philosophical framework may be built. That basic form of all fiction called the short story precedes any intricate novel, as parts proceed a whole, and yet both are founded upon the author's penetrating internal insight and its exposition through the interaction of the fictional characters. In any short story we have psychological analysis applied to subjective insight, but, of course, we also have merely intriguing storytelling derived from the writer's art. These internal insights into the structure of existence, made into an art form, constitute the philosophical basis for a literature which might lend substance to both metaphysics and theology.

There are, to be sure, several elements in any literary form which are not quite a revelation of existence and which depend upon no necessary internal insight. These are suspense, motion towards a climax (upon which much of the storyteller's art rests), the knack of graphic description, and many others. That the literary art form contains so many nonphilosophical elements has often obscured our vision in discerning its crucial philosophical aspects. Its power to represent man's inner life in its interrelationships by presenting it as external action or by reducing thought to word has often gone unnoticed in an externally oriented philosophical age. Heidegger, however, discerned at least something of this quality in poetry, and Kierkegaard concentrates on the importance of aesthetic form.

This variety of elements prevents any literary form from ever being a perfectly pure philosophical instrument. Besides, literature always portrays psychological states which have varying degrees of significance, and therefore the story form could never in every respect or in every instance be of philosophical import; e.g., as when the mood is one simply of lighthearted enjoyment. Among the principles for a philosophically formed novel, there are only a few which actually have the required revealing power (e.g., Camus, *The Stranger* or *The Plague;* most classical Greek drama; and *Job*). For instance, a plot which involves "moral perplexity," in which "death brings a peculiar transformation of character," etc., actually provides in literature the means to reveal an inner life, and these crucial examples are sufficient to give substance to a philosophical psychology drawn from literature. Paralleling what Plato said of his Forms: if in ourselves or in others the inner life could be discerned with only the naked eye or simply by itself, literature would be merely entertaining, lacking philosophical import. There is, in fact, a literature of genuine philosophical import, and the question arises, *How is it possible that it should be able to perform this task?*

Furthermore, the word *literature* may mean an exploration of psychological states, whereas in the usual sense it often merely denotes the interesting modes of activity which describe the existence characteristic of fictional characters. If we consider fiction merely the material, philosophical literature becomes "the description of psychological states of metaphysical significance." And with this only are we now concerned. States which can never have metaphysical significance, but are remembered only for their literary elegance, would not require us to turn to fiction to build a philosophy. These alone would never provide us with the necessary material; they would reveal no metaphysically basic structure. Consequently, we have to form for ourselves a list of psychological states which are revealed in fiction, the philosophical import of which can actually be discerned. That is, we have to learn whether they actually refer to basic psychological structures in human nature or merely to entertaining creations of the author's imagination.

To describe what a psychological state can be that is not of metaphysical significance would take us away from the basis of philosophy, and we are not here concerned with the unphilosophical aspects of life. Both life and literature are full of trivia. The crucial and the revealing are what we search for. We should investigate only the insight to be derived from a philosophical literature, the actuality of which can be confirmed in any classic dramatic presentation of life. Through this, knowledge becomes possible for the reader without his necessarily passing through that experience himself, except through vicariously sharing the experience available in the literature. Literature not only makes inner structure overt by defining it through interactions; it extends our own experience beyond its individual limits. One interesting conclusion can now be drawn: All the universal aspects of human existence are seldom known directly in any daily life, but they can eventually be experienced in literary form.

Literature and Moral Life

The formal aspect of literature which is crucial here is the structure of moral activity as it is revealed within psychological states when explored literarily. To be known without the reader's personal experience, they must be structures basic enough to all experience to be grasped by extension. A vicarious experience of significance depends on the reference in the reader's grasp to a comparable basic structure in his own life, and this requires metaphysical discernment. Inquiry here extends, not to the special and isolated aspects of human nature, the properties of which seem philosophically unimportant, but to psychological states and to human interaction of metaphysical significance; i.e., situations within which some basic structure of human nature is grasped.

The complex of these is what we properly designate as philosophical literature. If the possibility of extracting knowledge from literature which contains a philosophical psychology is in question, our problem is this: "How can we know that the moral activity of human beings, represented in their interacting inner psychological states, will ever form configurations of metaphysical significance?" Or we could phrase it thus: "How is it possible to know that the specific configurations found in the forms of moral activity in fictional life will ever reveal structures which are basic for all psychological states in general?"

The solution of the problem, presented in either way, amounts to the same thing for the point at issue, namely, the metaphysical significance of literature. The revelatory forms of human activity, under which alone a penetrating knowledge of the structures common to human beings is possible, actually describe all human beings in the interaction of their psychological states. Human beings in isolation or in public view are not considered here, since our task is to structure and thus to reveal the inner life of man.

Is this all summed up if we say: "A clarification of the meaning of human existence can never be derived solely from the internal life as each person knows it in himself. Private existence simply does not have that clarity. (The conclusions of the preceding chapter were provisional only. Now a new condition is added.) And this is known to be true whenever a critical decision is required of me; moral clarity is made possible only by some significant experience other than my own which illuminates the choices open to me. Everything which a dramatic presentation of life teaches us as decisive for existence comes from an internal insight based on interpersonal relations and their ethical resolution, now isolated and made concrete in literary structure." Facing life's final hour with Camus' *Stranger,* we too can decide "to start life all over again." [1]

Before personally experiencing each psychological state, we can come to discern those elements of human nature through which, alone, clarity about the internal life is made possible. Of course, this never extends to all the endless forms of activity to which

1 Albert Camus, *The Stranger* (New York: Vintage Books, 1956), p. 154.

human beings might be subject, the detail of which is as infinite as it is uninteresting and discloses no basic psychological state. We study literature by extracting the elements of human nature. The reactions of one human being on another are the only means of revelation or added insight. Alone and individually, we cannot arrive at such an internal and dramatic grasp of the inner nature of man. Psychological insight needs the addition of literary intrapersonal structure. Descartes should be told: An individual meditation is a wrong approach to philosophy.

A literature of philosophic content renders inner structure visible, and in this way its metaphysical basis is rendered meaningful. We examine, accordingly, the metaphysical elements of human nature through their psychological states which have been given crucial literary import. For if I could simply by choosing see a priori the elements of human nature without the medium of literature, I might easily fall into error and fancy that I simply saw life's basic (metaphysical) structures through a simple inspection of my own life. Then I might move around in endless circles in a vain internal search for the structures of moral activity which can be extended to all of human nature; but this, simple individual inspection alone can never give me. Despite a common misconception, the structures of human life are not easily discerned. Although they are not overt, they can be made graphic in literary form. (The difference here may perhaps be compared to that between individual *vs.* group therapy.)

The fiction written by the existentialists involves the whole complex of human psychological states in their interaction, and this gives it particular philosophic meaning. Here we are not concerned with the procedures for criticising any literature already constructed, for this presupposes a grasp of the technical structures to be analyzed by the literary critic. Our issue concerns how, through the internal life and the ability it gives us to identify with others, we can study the structure of moral activity as it is presented in literary forms.

Most often these are not forms of activity known as such in our own overt experience, since they would yield us no literary insight of real philosophical import if they simply presented moral structure as it is generally observed. We want to ask how the elements of human nature, grasped by the reader vicariously through literature for metaphysics, come from the same sources from which any writer must derive all the possible reactions that one human being may have upon another. If every author actually draws from the same pool of common structures, every metaphysical reader can discover a common base too.

In the first place, although the clarification of the meaning of existence based upon some penetrating dramatic insight has its source in the author's grasp of psychological principles, all clarification of existence is not derived solely from literature. Besides dramatic insight, and the psychological insight presented in literature, some special penetrating experience must be added in each individual reader's case. The same piece of literature does not make the same impact on every reader, but is this necessary additional experience something that is within our control?

These revealing human experiences have their source in the philosophical impact which psychology can have when derived from a powerful form of inner self-reflection. All other insights must first of all be assimilated to this center and then, by means of the individual's grasp of himself, either be changed into the discernible structures of dramatic form or else taken from it. Presented dramatic meaning must first have been grasped internally—though not necessarily externally—in the author's inner psychic life. When the reader or listener grasps this meaning, he can return to the author's source of experience and enter in after him.

The Dramatic Clarification of Existence

Any clarification of existence, so far as it is applicable to all human beings, is also related to some powerful, special, and unsettling experience in which the reader is involved and to which he attaches meaning. Those experiences which are applicable only to a few individuals are merely insights without general philosophical import. They require no basic situation productive of intense self-reflection, but only the logical connection of miscellaneous insights by discursive reason via the author's loose pen. But any universally applicable clarification always requires, besides the signs and results of psychological insight, the addition of special situations originally drawn out of inner self-reflection. This makes possible the application to all human beings of this powerful but seemingly isolated personal insight. The source from which the profound author draws is also our common source; what a reading or a hearing does is invite us to return thence once again.

Inner self-revelation is at first without philosophical import. It holds good only for our own situation, unless it is extended. Not until afterward do we give it a new reference—i.e., relate it to a basic psychological condition—and then we can perceive that it will always hold good for us and for everyone else in a similar state. For whenever an inner self-revelation reflects a common psychological condition, all other concepts concerning the same psychological state must also agree among themselves basically in what they reflect. Thus the application to all human beings of a powerful but isolated insight signifies nothing else than that it actually has revealed a form or a structure of common human moral interaction. That is, it reveals not merely a relation of our individual insights to some particular psychological condition, but a characteristic of any crucial psychological condition as such. There would be no reason for an inner self-revelation of any other man necessarily to agree with mine, if it were not for a common psychological condition from which they all arise and with which they accord; hence they can agree with one another because of the basis to which they refer and from which they are drawn. Dramatic insight unites us in its source, and this is a unity which is not possible in public life and action.

Therefore, applicability to all human beings and the power to reveal forms of human moral interaction are equivalent concepts. We cannot know psychological conditions without being given some direct material; yet when we consider that any powerful self-revelation in fiction illuminates human moral interaction and thus yields some understanding, we know it to have applicability to all human beings. By such a basic fictional self-revelation of structure, we come to know our own psychological states, though these remain unknown insofar as they might occur when connected with particular facts. We connect these literary insights with our own experienced insights, already derived from our own particular pattern of human interaction.

The general psychological state always remains unknown when taken by itself. But when a situation is powerful enough to produce an undistorted self-reflection, the connection of the results which such inner reflection gives to our insight can be found to be applicable to all human beings. The psychological condition is thus made significant by dramatic illustration. "To know" need not mean to experience directly and publicly. Thus, fictional self-revelation is rendered applicable to all human beings by the powerful context which literature provides for concrete grasp. A reader reads alone but understands in common. Alone, with Camus we experience *The Fall*.

To illustrate the matter: when we say, "I feel happy," or "Silence moves me to reflection, but activity obscures understanding," we express internal conditions which are valid only for the individual. I do not at all expect that I or any other person shall always find it as I now do. Each of these states expresses only a relation of two moods within the same individual—that is, myself—and then only as it is in my present state of reflection. Consequently, they are not generally revealing of human moral structure. These are psychological states without philosophical import. Penetrating and intense insights can be of quite a different nature. What the internal life teaches me under certain circumstances of crucial significance it could always teach me and everybody; and its applicability to human beings is limited neither to the individual nor to his state at a particular time.

In this respect the inner self-revelations in fiction of basic structure are potentially applicable to all human beings. For instance, when I say "The self is vulnerable," this self-reflection can be a revelation of general insight too. One instance may be sufficient to reveal this to me, and this can be in dramatic form rather than in some overt experience. If it is a penetrating and forceful insight of significance which is mediated through literature, this connection should be seen under a condition which reveals some structure of human nature. I understand, therefore, that I and every other reader should always derive the same insight from the same element of human nature. When such an insight comes in literary form, literature has an unmistakable philosophic import.

We must analyze the internal life evident in a literary piece to see what in it can produce an insight into human existence and is able to induce self-reflection. How can a penetrating or sometimes isolated but powerful insight possibly become universally significant? The foundation here is an insight in which I become fully self-conscious; that is, one in which I grasp the psychological principles regulating the various forms which human existence may take, and actually does take, in me. Next, there can be an interior self-revelation only from a situation that induces and stimulates self-reflection.

This self-revelation may be twofold: first, I may merely compare insights and connect them to refer only to a consciousness of my particular state; or, second, I may extend them to a consciousness of human life in general. The former self-revelation is merely a reflection of miscellaneous particular and perhaps autobiographical insights, and hence it is of subjective validity only. It is merely a connection of insights into my present mental state, or into that of the dramatic character without reference to any basic psychological or moral structure. Thence arises no revelation concerning the moral reaction of one human being upon another of sufficient depth to be of philosophical assistance. The insight is immediate only.

Quite another kind of inner self-reflection therefore is required before any insight can be seen as revealing a basic structure of all internal life. The literarily induced internal penetration of insight must reach to the reader's ethical consciousness and thereby procure valid structures for understanding human moral interaction—and then it must use this as a means to clarify human existence. A situation of this profundity gives a metaphysical significance to self-reflection. Let the intuition be that of an internal insight resulting from a firm moral resolution; then the importance of the insight becomes clear. For example, 'loyalty' may be seen as a necessary part of self-understanding. That is, the concept 'loyalty' as it adds meaning to individual action can be acquired through following characters in a fictional presentation. The situation produced by a dramatic insight based on resolution is a basic human structure discovered in the self-reflection which literature induces, and this may be totally disparate from all external examination of psychological states and actions. It serves to make possible a valid form for understanding loyalty as a human moral situation that is extendable to all.

Self-Reflection, the Inner Life, and Insight

Before an inner insight can come from a penetrating and concrete situation provided by literature, its importance in striking deep enough in human nature to grasp its structure should be emphasized. For instance, loyalty comes to be understood in a situation in which dramatic insight is based on firm resolution. Our understanding is increased by an addition of meaningfulness through which fictional loyalty is discovered but not merely in the insight into loyalty derived from my present state or from several states of mine. It must be from the insight derived in some fictional situation structured in such a way that it assuredly produces personal meaning whenever the writer can make loyalty become real. This inner way of understanding, e.g., "Loyalty makes insignificant action meaningful," becomes a valid form for grasping the connection that defines our human moral structure. It requires an insight both penetrating and concrete, because such loyalty can spring only from an inner condition. Since it cannot be derived from the external circumstances, it is best revealed by the writer's literary skill in portraying inner situations, in this case one of resolution.

This makes clear the importance of fictional insight, since our only means for an involvement in loyalty may be as it is made clear in the dramatic situation. In fiction an insight may be based on dramatic resolution, and this the novel or play provides, whereas our problem in life is that our moral situations often continue without resolution and thus provide no insight. Fiction makes possible what life may not allow. Thereby authors can make insights significant, not merely with respect to historical circumstances, but with respect to the basis for our self-understanding in general. In this way literature turns an individual clarification of existence into a valid form for understanding all human moral interaction, because it provides the concrete basis so necessary for the first grasp which our own lives may not provide.

If an inner self-reflection is to be extended to become applicable to all human beings, the basic synthesis necessary never consists of merely particular insights connected by comparisons and turned into cumulative experience. Insight would be impossible were not a situation productive of self-reflection superimposed on the dramatic plot which later could be abstracted by the reader's insight. For example, the principle, "Depression results from a feeling of the absurd and the consequent loss of meaning," presupposes that depression has its importance made clear from a particular situation that requires important ethical decision. (See Camus' discussion in *The Rebel*.) This serves to make significant the insight into how depression results from a loss of meaning induced through the medium of psychological impact; that is, emotion. For drama contains, it is true, emotion sufficient to induce the depth of psychological penetration necessary.

To be proved, then, the possibility of a metaphysics extended from the internal life must be seen to rest upon basic situations that produce a depth of self-reflection. The various functions of the moods of self-reflection must run parallel to these instances of intense dramatic heights, or such situations will be nothing more than entertainment. To be philosophically fruitful, dramatic situations must contain the situation in which the self may be revealed to itself through the medium of one or more of the characters. This is known to the reader in his solitary state and yet it is universally extendable. Hereby also the concrete principles of the structure of all internal life are made clear by the diagnoses given by the author as he expands his plot. What the author must grasp to write with any profundity, the reader must also grasp to understand, and this he does internally and vicariously; by insight he participates in universal meaning. Without this the author writes trivia and the reader is unmoved.

Classical Qualities and Philosophical Importance

Now we are in a position to comment on what it is that transforms certain pieces of literature into classics. Compared with the avalanche of words written and read, plays acted and seen, only a minute portion is preserved, remembered, and transmitted. Yet that small part is valued beyond its comparative bulk. Strictly speaking, there is not enough difference in the plots used or in the material and situations described to account for this extreme discrimination. Much of this selectivity, of course, is due to the author's skill, i.e., his power and control over the dramatists' and novelists' art.

Here the literary critic must help us grasp the variety, since great literature falls into no single form but into multitudinous literary molds. Yet beyond the author's skill—and some great writers are comparatively poor craftsmen—more is needed to account for the difference between writing which is preserved and the much more vast bulk of literature which is forgotten. The focus of attention is always only on a small portion of what is and has been written, and simple inspection does not reveal enough difference in the content to explain this discrimination sufficiently.

Perhaps the greater part of any given literary or dramatic classic is not extraordinary. Even more perplexing, we must try to account for the fact that many of the works produced by great authors are poor. What makes a work great and gives it literary immortality is perhaps the exploration of some insight, and finally its stabilization through infused verbal structure, into a universally applicable moral situation. This insight is not to be found in the external circumstances of the work (since these things men never share), but in man's inner life. Some moral perplexity with which man struggles internally but can never fully resolve externally, or into which he cannot induce stable structure in his own inner life, is at some moment brought into clear focus by the author. On the stage or in the novel, the words used produce a structure which the reader or listener may grasp and apply internally—seldom if ever externally.

To the dismay of empiricists, universality can never be found by external inspection; customs separate us all. Our own inner moral life constantly seeks expression and is structured in overt action that is only partially under our control. It can never stabilize itself or produce its own clarity or free itself from changing moods. The author of classical proportion can do this, at least at times, and we respond to that ability in him, although the bulk of his work may have no greater structural clarity than that of the legion of his forgotten colleagues. We are first given an existing philosophical structure and then we proceed. We do not philosophize from ourselves. We are able to do so only by having bits of previous thought introduced into us. Similarly, we cannot structure our own inner life. In literature we find this accomplished in such a way that it forms in us a certain clarity and the beginning of some structure. Significant thought is induced only by the irritation of foreign matter, just as pearls are produced by a grain of sand.

To comprise this whole matter in one idea, it is first necessary to remind the reader that we are discussing, not the origin of the internal life, but an understanding of what lies within it, and this through literary presentation. The former pertains to analytic psychology, although even so it could never be adequately explained without the latter, which takes the pieces of the inner life as these flow from its sources and embodies them in concrete structure. Whatever its origin, our internal life is not structured as it arises, a fact which is the cause of most psychic difficulty. Structuring is our problem, and when literature accomplishes this crucial process it has great psychological value.

Our self-understanding connects the grasp of psychological principles, insofar as they are given in dramatic insight, while the author's self-understanding must express what a dramatic view of life in general contains. The would-be author cultivates insights which possess literary validity and which are not so much a product of what and how much he experiences himself as of the metaphysical depth of his self-reflection. Those special and unique insights, which may even be derived from exotic circumstances, add to a general dramatic insight. They speed its logical connection into some basic self-revelation and this is why a would-be author may often profit most from unusual experiences.

Yet there must be something within the author's inner life too which quietly guides the synthesis of self-revealing moments to yield a clear structure and valid forms for understanding human moral interaction. The internal situation must be such that insight is made significant because that author is constituted for depth penetration, and this then results in revelation rather than in merely reporting another interesting incident. The classical author's own internal structure produces synthetical unity of crucial insights, which can then be transformed by his technical skill into a self-revelation that can be presented in a literary fashion. The same experiences do not always produce a classic work; the author's inner nature makes the difference.

The sum of the matter is this: the business of human existence is to seek insight, sometimes through a literature that induces self-reflection, while the business of discursive reason is to analyze these experiences. The union of these evidences given through insight only occurs if some basic self-understanding is present both in author and in reader. Reading good literature does not necessarily enlighten everyone. Analyzing a dramatic presentation of life, therefore, requires the same self-reflection that its original authorship demanded for its composition. Hence the author's self-revelation is sometimes merely momentary and entertaining. Then insights are noted in passing and are enjoyed, but they do not become the occasion for internal penetration. On the other hand, literary revelation may be applicable to all human beings if the author's insights are united in a structure of force sharp enough to penetrate to life's base.

The psychological function of all self-revelation by the characters in fiction is but one way of structuring the inner life in a way that it may then be grasped. But if the author's insight is strong enough to mold specific dramatic situations, these situations will always yield the same insight to any attentive listener and so are principles capable of application to all human beings, whether grasped by all or not. This union of insights is either analytical, probing for further meaning, or synthetical, combining and adding various evidences and insights one to another to add clarity through structure. Life as revealed in drama consists in this synthetical connection of glimpses (insights) into a single consciousness so far as the author may discern and the reader follow. Hence, in the optimum situation all insights fall together in a structure that is made clear. The synthetical unity producible by dramatic insight is evident when the reader discovers a form which is now valid for understanding some aspect of all human moral interaction.

The union of insight brought to consciousness through a literary mode of presentation is a valid procedure for all life. These procedures, insofar as they result in a union yielding clear structure, are also operative in any creative work. Insofar as they cannot be deduced from life's overt and ordinary procedures, they provide ethical directives just to the extent that one understands the synthetic activity at the base of all creative effort. Yet no element basic to human nature which is brought to light in a special fictional insight can be grasped without a self-reflection strong enough also to alter our own inner structure. The reader must be molded now as the character was first shaped by the author, and both modifications come as a result of the author's ability to penetrate our inner life. There are therefore literary and dramatic principles of meaningful structure which act in a way that further develops the internal life, and these structures are capable of presentation in literary form. They are "words made into form altering flesh."

The Literary Author and Philosophical Grasp

The principles for forming meaningful structures in the life of literature are grasped by the author in developing the reactions of one character on another as these grow in his literary imagination, and this can be known only as a result, never in advance. Thus our major question is: "How is it possible for literature to be relevant to philosophy?" and we have only one possible answer. For the form required for the authorship of literature with philosophical import is actually one which every author must discover and learn to follow if he is to be successful. Authors build characters and situations by discovering structure and following its development. Whenever this coincides with some classical mold, a basic element in human nature has been given verbal form. These literary forms constitute a psychological structure firm enough to yield insight and, eventually, understanding, although such birth is never accomplished without pain. Previous structures must yield or be altered if new life is to be possible. Reader and author are often united both by the pain and the pleasure of insight. The reader makes the same discoveries of form and relationship later that the author did originally.

The situations which contain an insight into the elements of human nature, now synthetically structured for dramatic self-revelation, constitute a possible metaphysical basis. Finally, the principles by means of which all insights have their importance made clear in a literary situation constitute the plot form for a novel. A literary plot proceeds from an internal grasp of literary characters, and it makes possible a control of their developing relations. If it in strictness controls the moral reactions of one human being on another so that clear structure results in verbal form, it can produce literature of philosophical significance. Insight into the elements of human nature, if given form in a plot, can uncover the same foundations which metaphysics seeks and upon which it rests. Such, in brief, is the first conclusion of this investigation.

The first necessity in writing a novel is to make clear the importance of all dramatic situations; for example, insights into anxiety or dread during a period of psychological impact. Only if its importance is made clear can the situation become an ethical directive—i.e., an application of philosophical psychology to the life of literature. Second, the author must make clear the importance of a penetrating psychological insight within the life of the drama itself so that the action reflects a grasp of psychological principles which denotes real insight and does not seem arbitrary. Not that there is always a strong moral impact on the reader; the power in any state is not always released upon the reader, but it may be. The reader, for example, may actually "feel" the presence of evil in Sartre's *The Condemned of Altona.*

Yet there is, between strong moral impact and a total void of insight, some degree of psychological impact on the reader or observer. Between every given degree of light and darkness, pain and absolute pleasure, sorrow and absolute happiness, involvement in anxiety and total oblivion to dread, diminishing levels can be conceived. In exactly the same manner, between psychological darkness and clarity there are ever diminishing degrees which obtain, and this tells us why psychological struggle cannot end while life lasts. The degree may lessen but the oppositions continue.

Hence, for instance, there is no insight which can prove that absolute non-being exists. For there is no psychological darkness that cannot be considered a consciousness which is outbalanced only by a stronger darkness and thus still contains some hope of light. Man could not experience absolute non-being and live, which is at least as convincing a proof that non-being does not exist as Plato's argument in the *Parmenides.* Insight occurs in all instances through a grasp of psychological principles, and so the literary mode built upon this comprehension can cause the reader to anticipate even actual human existence. Through dramatic self-reflection the observer can anticipate human moods as yet unexperienced, by means of an ethical structure which is uncovered. We learn that life can be lived in this way. Consequently the reality in all literary insight has universal extendability, but only when subjectively grasped and applied to inner structure. This is the application of philosophical psychology to a literature which has genuine philosophical significance, since the result is to reduce us to the root of all existence.

If we examine all literary insight with a view to uncovering the possible modes of existence, its significance is apt to be, not psychological, but philosophical. No insight can ever be applicable to all human beings if it does not involve the inner ethical directives by which such dramatic insight first became possible and then could be structured into a classical mold. Hence literary insight must first have its importance made clear under a situation of crisis, and this leads us to believe that the dramatic situation is that foundation which actually gives significance to all of existence. Drama, whether comedy or tragedy, rests upon meaning, and thus meaning can be apprehended through it.

Repetition is found among literary forms (e.g., repeated plots), and human action is known via literature to involve constant repetition. (Cf. Kierkegaard's stress on the value of *Repetition*.) Penetrating and clarifying insights do not appear only under the guise of sheer novelty. Skillful authors transform familiar situations into new sources of insight, sometimes by the very use of repetition. The possibility of fostering understanding through a dramatic picture of life—by connecting psychological states as they are portrayed in literature—depends upon a situation of moral seriousness which repetition can portray. These ethical directives are the real forms which are discernible in serious literature and make its discovered structure applicable to us all.

Finally, a knowledge of the meaning and the connection of personal insights in a work of literature and of their significance for human life in general is recognized by the reader only in what is for him, of necessity, an isolated insight. Reading or listening to discern meaning is always an individual affair. Consequently, the relation of insight to the life of drama combines possibility, actuality, and freedom, since we never find one insight which reveals that life can proceed in only one way for all actors or all readers. The novel is most effective for distinguishing truth when its action reveals that the elements do not necessitate a single outcome; i.e., when the reader is left in some suspense and understands that several conclusions may be drawn.

Ethical Directives and Literary Insight

The ethical directives drawn from the literary method show life's inherent possibilities; for example, life might be lived in some different manner regardless of whether the world approves it or whether any individual decides to accept it. A perfectly fulfilled drama is complete in the sense that there are no more ethical directives to be found within it. This affords a satisfaction which can never be attained in real life, since it allows no such exhaustion. Yet this is not all; the components involved in the ethical directives hold still in a manner never found true in our own life, and thus they yield a clarity which is unavailable in actual existence. We may not be able to live in that way in fact, but we clearly see that it could be done.

We ought to bear in mind the premise which makes this dramatic grasp possible and at the same time limits the application of such ethical directives: the author, although he explores real connections, is always at liberty to alter relations or to bypass intervening steps in a way that our own existence does not allow. Such insight, then, is ethically clarifying, but at the same time it is often not immediately and directly applicable, since a certain unreality is necessary to produce such clarity. Our conclusion: The artificial may be made more clear than the actual.

Literary ethical insights, then, contain only the conditions which clarify inherent possibilities. To the degree that its conditions are not ours, the insights may clarify but not necessarily aid specific actions. Consequently, I do not say that every human being will experience in literature an immediate and beneficial psychological impact. His own internal reality may possess a degree of similarity, but just to the extent that he focuses on a connection of accidental factors in a subject, he may miss the universally applicable structure and grasp only the factors of unreality or difference. This no author, however powerful, can control, because a synthetical connection that forms insight is not possible without reference to the observer's psychological state and to his own understanding of his existence. The essential limitation of the dramatic situation in producing ethical insights is that all human beings *may* react and follow the author to the extreme depths, but they do this only insofar as they themselves are able to experience the interaction of the psychological states.

Hence there follows a peculiar mode of proof of literary principles. They do not directly validate themselves by always producing literary insight and thus leading every reader to the same conclusion. This depends on whether each of us develops a genuine internal life of his own; literary insights constitute only the stimulus, never the specific form. This is an ultimate limitation. Again, insofar as the literary insight contains human moods and psychological states, there is always within a mood an ever decreasing transition from extremes to the total disappearance of the mood, and this makes its impact on the receiver (audience or reader) difficult to control.

The reality within a given literary insight must vary to some extent, so that any particular human mood, e.g., *the growth of anxiety and dread, does not itself inspire every reader.* If this were not so, different actors could not find in the moods of one role the varying interpretations given by each new acting generation. A good actor grasps the ranges included by a skillful author in his words. Still, the transition—e.g., from the absence of anxiety and the absence of dread to the full realization of dread—depends upon the actor's (or reader's) own response and upon whether he knows dread himself.

Consequently, human moral decisiveness can come about only if the author is successful in opening up some aspects of dread against which we have heretofore been protected. Yet, as a meaningful structure of life is unfolded in the dramatic presentation, it can result in a psychological impact of insight, but only to the extent that the author is able to make his words uncover some depth latent within his reader too. Hence the necessary involvement of philosophical psychology in literature, since it is by psychological impact alone that literature is able to present valid insights to us.

Above all, the reader must pay attention to the author's unfolding of the ethical insight. The full impact may be lost if the subtlety of the connection is missed. For the genesis of insight is central to its existence in the life of drama. Making existence meaningful, say through producing an experience of dread, is one way to insure moral activity in which, alone, the addition of meaning comes to all human beings. But how this comes about in its origins the reader must understand too. Then a genuine and believable fictional life can add depth to his own existence.

Since these are only prolegomena for a contemporary metaphysics to be expounded, I cannot yet produce the finished product itself. Owing to the severe critique of metaphysics in the
modern era, my reader has probably long consented to consider
the dramatic presentation of life as a mere internalization of
external description and insight, and hence he has not
considered that the life of drama might go much beyond this,
even to provide a support for metaphysics. It imparts a
clarification of existence through valid insights into an understanding of human moral interaction, and for this purpose it
builds upon an internal grasp of the basic constituents of
existence. Thus, we should pay special attention to the literary
description of life, not as a mere aggregate of external insights,
but as a revelation of the inner life which can in turn make
external existence become clear.

A New Meaning for Philosophy

Now we are prepared to remove the hesitancy which hinders
some from accepting Kierkegaard as a philosopher. He justly
maintains that we cannot comprehend by reason the possibility
of ethical insight based merely on conventional patterns; that is,
the objective relation of the decisions of one human being to the
decisions made by others. For this makes ethical life appear to be
external. What we must comprehend is the concept of existence
as it is made meaningful by inner resolution. This is the view
that at the foundation of the existence of human beings there lies
a subjective resolution which cannot itself be the product of any
other human being's reported experience. We cannot even form
a notion of the possibility of such a meaning of experience unless
we grasp the principles which govern the structure of the novel,
together with the internal insights which alone cause it to be
profound, and the way in which this inner process illumines our
own existence.

The very same incomprehensibility affects the way in which we
view the community of human beings. It is, for instance, difficult
to see how a crisis arising from our own separate existence could

involve others who are not overtly in the same circumstances. But I am far from believing that these crucial ethical situations are ever derived from the external life. The structure and conflict in literature are not imaginary, a mere illusion produced in us by the creative author; on the contrary, I have tried to show that the ethical directives derived from literary crises are firmly grounded in and drawn from our inner life. The basis may be the same in the author and in the reader and may have its value in applicability to all human beings. This is the metaphysical basis of ethics.

I have no idea how a community can exist between human beings if they are left in isolation or how men can act on individual insight based on isolated resolution. Men cannot stand in community with others unless they are bound together as members of a genuine group. Dramatic situations do not contain simply what is discovered in subjective insight alone, but such self-reflection must think of its relationship to others. We have to form a connection of individuals to be able to carry on dramatic self-reflection which can produce a basic understanding of the individual-in-a-group. Indications of the inner state appear, in one sort of literary self-analysis, as revelatory of the individual's relation to any crisis situation; in another, as decision in preparation for action; and, in a third, as partial glimpses which form a possible total internal grasp of the whole self in its relations to others. If we follow the development of this style, we learn what it means to live in community.

If left alone we can have no knowledge applicable to all psychological states, since our own objective situation is not wide enough in itself to yield such desired insights. If I should concern myself with one psychological state in itself, there is not a single possible attribute by which I could know that it might make existence significant in any life other than my own. Only under the impact of a crisis, it seems, is our inner life made clear and our self brought into community with others. Alone, I cannot understand myself, since the inner self is inexplicable in isolation. Only literature can objectify our inner selves and relate us one to another. That is its power and its occasional rare glory.

Of course, no dramatic situation offers the possibility of

making such a connection clear for all aspects of existence at once. How can human beings involved in the psychological states of a dramatic life experience literary situations which together induce a self-reflection that reveals the significance of existence? If it could be made clear that here I grasp not only the possibility but also the reality of my inner life, the importance of literary insight would also be clear. These dramatic situations are vicarious experiences that provide ethical directives for building a meaningful internal life of our own. Could we gain insight into ourselves through overt actions alone, the philosophical role of literature would not exist.

To test Kierkegaard's psychological life situation (his *crux metaphysicorum*) —i.e., the rule that dramatic insight makes possible a moral resolution—we must first see how by means of literary psychology the basis for a possible self-structuring is given. In other words, we must grasp how some dramatic state serves as an antecedent to the resolution and to the inner insight that is the consequence of the resolution. But it is possible that in such insight we may meet with a metaphysical basis for human relations which runs thus: that certain literary structures are capable of providing insight that is available in no other way, the inner life being assessable only indirectly, never directly. If this is so, we must use the revelations which fictional characters can give to us to supplement and extend our own overt experience.

For instance, we may say that if perplexity lasts long enough it paralyzes moral action. This may not be clear from our own meager experience, but it may be revealed with clarity in some dramatic situation. In *Hamlet,* for example, we have an addition of meaning precisely because of a situation based on the lack of resolution. The diagnosis derived from this play would be that perplexity is responsible for paralyzing moral action because of the insecurity which it produces. This connection can be laid bare in literature and serve as a ground for insight in the reader, whereas his own life is inadequate for the purpose because of its confusion in immediacy and detail. Direct experience may obscure rather than clarify, which if true frustrates the hope of the strict empiricist.

How is dramatic insight based on moral resolution? Most

important is the possibility for human beings to achieve a general insight based on observing moral resolution. The situation explicating such resolution reveals an element of human nature visible only to a skilled observer and master of dramatic technique. Such a dramatic bit abstracted from life can be helpful only as literary insight is made applicable to all human beings via the meaning added when its structure is grasped.

Hence if the basic situations producing self-reflection are present in the psychological states of dramatic life, they may apply to human beings as an avenue which opens their search for meaning. They serve, as it were, only to underscore our own momentary and mixed instinctive dramatic insight. Beyond this and as external directives for overt action they are arbitrary combinations without objective reality, and we can neither know their possible application nor verify—or even render intelligible by any example—their reference to overt social states. Their further insight can come only from metaphysics, and consequently the situations produced by the psychological insight of literature can be extended further only within a metaphysical scheme. Drama is metaphysic's prolegomenon.

To its originators, existentialism may not have seemed to provide the solution to Kierkegaard's problem, i.e., how within an individual one might find situations such that they can be the origin of metaphysics. The structure and insight which we have discovered as necessary in its construction adds a depth of meaning to literature which never occurred to Kierkegaard—that to be an author of significance requires metaphysical depth as well as artistic agility. The author of drama grasps life, and he derives a meaning from his grasp of man's basic situation that can then produce self-reflection in his reader. The metaphysical author of fiction provides an insight not contained in any surface description or observation of the same circumstances.

There is, therefore, one result of all our foregoing inquiries: "All ethical conclusions are derived from the metaphysical explorations of a possible internal life," one often made overt by an author. These conclusions, however, can never be taken as a description of human beings in ordinary public life. Our ethical understanding often rests on a literary insight derived from exploring psychological states within the life of drama. Hence philosophical psychology, as well as literature with philosophical import, can be produced only by an individual of unique internal penetration who has the ability to make overt his findings through the medium of words. Literature can provide the basic insight and much of the meaning for metaphysics, but never the metaphysics in technical form. Without the grasp of inner structure which literature can provide, metaphysics is without real foundation; with it, once again it is significant, although still lacking technical structure.

Insight and Observation

The naturalist who admits only disinterested observation, the man who believes he can decide matters of metaphysics and theology without any genuine involvement, may feel that any insight which is internally derived cannot have objective validity. Metaphysics must make sense to more than one man; so the issue is whether the author unfolds an inner structure which actually is common to all. What is internal at least *may* be universal, whereas what is externally observed can never be. With all our disinterested observation we can never comprehend the latent meaning within a dramatic presentation of life. But when anyone is questioned individually about his observational principles, he must grant that there are many of them which he has not taken simply from experience as the eye sees it, and which are therefore based upon an inner grasp of the situation that is not available to anyone who lacks equal profundity.

Our problem, however, is that not every insight presented to one individual is available to every other person equally, and so only if another person actually shares the insight can it be proved to be there. Yet everyone has had an insight come—some penetration of inner structure induced by drama or literature—so that at least the process in general is known to be valid. Any individual insight may not produce the same effect in others; but through a series of attempts the effect which some have can at least be seen. We can understand what life without insight would be like, and we can know that our ethical problem concerns our inner life and not what can overtly be seen. Metaphysics has not found its base in the externally observed world, primarily because its source is not there. Our problems have their origin "beyond the physical," so that only a penetration into our inner life can locate metaphysics' source. Thus literature doth (might) make metaphysicians of us all.

Since the oldest days of philosophy, inquirers who have used disinterested observation have debated whether such a world may or may not have a structure sufficient to support metaphysical deductions. But it is also true that the world of insight, of which literature is our example, seems to indicate the existence of a noumenal world of greater solidity. Those who relied on external observation thought that literature dealt with a world of illusion, meaning that an author's insight could be considered only the product of his own imagination. Although we do not come to know human beings in this external way, however, we can know them through insights provided by a literary mode; for example, we see the way in which our human existence is affected by this unknown something, nonbeing (see chapter 6). The mode of philosophy, therefore, which assumes the possible validity of a literary insight, grants that human existence may actually find significance in having its very existence threatened. When existence is challenged to the core, then human nature is revealed. Our own protected lives may not be as revealing as that of an actor in a role of crisis.

This analysis still limits the ethical directives of the existentialist writings to this: that they shall not extend to all things—since everything would then be turned into mere literary insight—but that they shall hold good only for a metaphysics based on the psychological states discoverable in life depicted in literature. Reading develops moods which may induce self-reflection and insight, but the penetration gained is not into the organic and chemical structure of the world or even into men's objective relations. The existentialist insight leads into the inner human sphere. A metaphysics produced upon this basis, then, must show how nonsubjective metaphysical structures (e.g., nonbeing) can be known in their psychological impact (e.g., dread).

Still, our isolated situations of crisis, suffering, moral action, and inner reality can all become quite independent of the dramatic life, which through literature gives us an insight into human existence so that they actually can become fundamentally applicable to all human beings. What strengthens this conjecture is that the insight generated contains an assurance of significance in itself. The situation wherein a particular dramatic insight is based on moral resolution implies a procedure which extracts it from its setting and allows us to consider it alone. Metaphysically, we must then take over and abstract from this if we are to trace from it Being's structure. Literature opens avenues which metaphysics can then explore, but not until they have been opened for it.

Hence any situation productive of self-reflection often seems to have a deeper meaning and import than can be exhausted by its merely dramatic use, and so any induced self-reflection inadvertently adds to the house of the life of drama a much more extensive metaphysical wing. This it fills with structures of creative imagination, sometimes without realizing that it could not have penetrated Being's structure to this extent had not literary insight opened up the way.

At least one investigation therefore becomes indispensable where existentialist literature is concerned. This is to show that human existence can furnish the metaphysical context for the understanding of dramatic situations. The psychological state which produces insight actually occurs only in the dramatic situations of life, as the product of the artist's creative self-reflection upon incidents of insight. For our own self-reflection is only a faculty of insight. After the addition of meaning through insights found in literature, the corresponding metaphysical category begins to appear. The life of drama can therefore bring to light all the psychological states produced by existential situations; but before the isolated situations have any metaphysical significance, we must discover how a dramatically structured emotion is capable of penetrating Being's structure when neither individual experience nor empirical observation seems able to do so.

Imagination may perhaps be forgiven for occasional vagaries and for not keeping carefully within the limits of a presented dramatic structure, since it gains life and vigor by such flights and since it is always easier to moderate boldness than to stimulate languor. But metaphysical construction, which ought to *analyze* itself, can never be forgiven for indulging in vagaries. What we permit, encourage, and even depend upon in the artist we cannot allow in the metaphysical construction which follows him.

But the powers of metaphysical construction begin their development very innocently and modestly. They first bring to light the elementary structures inherent in us all before contact with a literary or a dramatic life, which yet require grounding upon material that can be found within the life of drama. Metaphysics later gradually drops these artistic limits. What is there to prevent this, since it quite freely began its original construction from them? It proceeds first from the newly found powers within literature, then moves to beings outside literature —in short, to a world for whose construction the materials have been available but simply not understood. Fertile fiction furnishes raw material abundantly, and the validity of metaphysics would be sustained and inspired by the dramatic life even if it had not begun there.

Answers to the Questions Posed

This question, what is the highest point that an existential metaphysics can ever reach and to which it must proceed for completion, really contains two questions.

First: How is literature in the philosophical sense, that is, in the sense of producing metaphysical insight, possible; how is it possible to reproduce anxiety, dread, and that which fills both—the underlying psychological states that produce human moods—in literature? The answer is: By means of the constitution of our insight into human existence, according to which it is in its own way affected by psychological states which are in themselves directly unknown to it and presented to us only in the form of literary insights. This answer is illustrated in Sartre's *Being and Nothingness* in the development of the origin of negativity, and in these Prolegomena by the solution offered to the problem of the present chapter (see also chapter 6).

Second: How is literature possible, in the philosophical sense, as the totality of techniques under which all literary insight must be presented to be grasped as adding meaning to the metaphysical enterprise? The answer might be this: It is only possible by means of the penetration of which self-reflection is capable. All the energy and depth of insight into human existence are assuredly directed to our own consciousness. By the same way in which we construct imaginatively (namely, by intuitive procedures), the dramatic life also is made possible, but its metaphysical extension must be clearly distinguished from an insight into the peculiarities of life's detail. This answer is illustrated in Kierkegaard's *Philosophical Fragments* in the "Interlude" (where he develops the relationship of being to non-being in a new way as a result of his psychological investigations) and in these Prolegomena in the course of the solution offered to the question of chapter 3 (for a development of this, see our Epilogue).

But how this peculiar property of our insight into human existence itself is made possible, or how our mode of self-reflection and of a dramatically based self-understanding can be its basis and also that of all psychological analysis, cannot be further probed or answered; it is a "first principle" which cannot be accounted for in terms other than itself. It is the meta-metaphysical basis for metaphysics; i.e., a psychologically fundamental condition. It is a fact, and upon this fact metaphysics is constructed. We can point it out, and have done so, but we cannot go behind it to explain it in terms of something else.

There are many powers of Being characterized in literature which we can experience only by means of our own dramatic sense. All of Being is by no means self-evident. Dramatic structuring makes insight possible, and the structure which we appropriate by our own sense is what makes drama possible. Experience cannot itself produce all of Being for our inspection, but on the other hand the important structures sometimes are clear only in literature and never in simple experience. Literature presents to us a totality which direct experience never could.

We understand literature only through knowing the structure which makes insight possible and by feeling its impact, and through that growing sensitive to its structure. And hence we can understand the forms of activity open to fictional characters only from the corresponding sense of ethical structure in us; that is, from the conditions for their potential embodiment in our own self-consciousness. This constitutes the awakening of an internal dramatic form of life in each observer and a deepening sensitivity to Being's possible structures still concealed in him and in his experience.

Even the main proposition expounded throughout this section —that the structured relation of one human being acting on another which literature exhibits can be a foundation for metaphysics—leads naturally to the proposition that the highest source of literature must lie in ourselves, insofar as our power of self-reflection can penetrate even to Being's nonevident side. We must seek to learn what reaction one person can produce on another in order to define that being's structure in literature; and conversely we must seek the sources of literature, as a valid form for understanding human activity which reveals the structure of Being. This depends upon our ability to gain insight into human existence and into our powers of self-reflection. For how could we otherwise discover these possible structures, since they are not directly the rules of empirical knowledge but are first of all synthetical extensions beyond overt experience? It seems at first strange, however certain it may be, to say: A human being's power of self-reflection does not derive its understanding of Being's structure from, but prescribes it to, literature.

We need not have actually experienced any particular anxiety to know, from its literary representation, that it is something to which we are subject by virtue of our humanity. If we consider the state of uncertainty by which this condition opens so many choices to us, we cannot avoid attributing a metaphysical status to this essentially clinical state. Two uncomplicated states of depression resulting from a general loss of meaning, for example, resemble each other in that both are characterized by uncertainty (however they may differ in circumstances) and are constituted so that the basic action leading to the resolution of one (i.e., decisiveness) will also produce the resolution of the other in spite of the different circumstances surrounding the origin of each.

The question now is: Does the loss of the power of activity originate in objective uncertainty, or does it really come from self-reflection? That is, does this state come into being independently of the power of self-reflection, owing to some discernible uncertainty, or is our own power of reflection itself really the cause? Does self-reflection which develops according to the situation (i.e., the particular effect of some depressing event on the individual) of itself introduce depression? Then, it is not the situation but our being which is the cause, and it is also, later, the cause of our insight and possible cure. Not an event, but our own lack of ethical decisiveness, is the real origin of depression, so that to overcome it we must look for insight into the same source.

When we follow the treatment implied by this analysis, we soon discern that it can be based only upon a condition in which self-reflection speeds the construction of the situation brought about by ethical indecision. The resulting effect is the depression of the individual, and we can enlarge this situation to include all humanity. Although conditions vary, ethical indecision is common to us all, so that in understanding depression based upon reflective uncertainty we grasp a structure of Being. All human beings are subject to the same fundamental elements of human nature. Even when the circumstances differ, we may still find that all the symptoms which the patient reports in depression—e.g., meaninglessness and loss of power—are similar (although not equal in degree) in the sense that they stem from some anxiety or dread common in all human existence. The explanation of a common psychological state which is found to be independent of individual circumstances leads us to discover its origin in the very structure of Being.

If we proceed still further to the fundamental teachings of existentialist theory, we find that a metaphysical explanation is applicable to all personalities in literature. Their circumstances are seldom ours, but their basic structure is. The symptoms decrease as the patient's basic anxiety is relieved; that is, as the extent of the grip of anxiety over the person is reduced. This fact seems to point out something necessarily inherent in the very nature of the human personality, and hence it is a metaphysically based knowledge. The sources of this now-discovered fact are simple; they merely rest upon the relation of indecision and uncertainty to basic anxiety. Its consequences are valuable as a basis for the metaphysical foundation of human nature inasmuch as Being is disclosed when the possible symptoms are manifest in the suffering of human beings. The relation which these possible symptoms have to one another means that understanding them depends more on a metaphysical grasp of the nature of Being, as it is manifest in human beings, than it does upon cataloging and describing particular events.

Here, accordingly, is a literature resting upon the ability of self-reflection to grasp the structure of Being. It builds chiefly from the kinds of reactions that one human being has on another, and it makes clear that the sources of anxiety are metaphysical and not empirical in their origin. Now we ask: Do the powers of literary construction themselves stem from anxiety, and does self-reflection learn what these are by merely endeavoring to uncover the enormous wealth of meaning that comes from understanding the metaphysical basis of anxiety? Or do these creative dramatic forms simply inhere in the power of self-reflection itself? In being forced to reflect after being seized by a psychological state, does one come automatically upon the elements in human nature which open the road to a metaphysical vision of Being's structure?

Anxiety is something so uniform, and in all its particular qualities so inexplicable, that we should certainly expect to find it as a basic theme for various kinds of literature. What makes anxiety metaphysically significant, when we bring to light its origin in ontological uncertainty or in the dread which comes from the recognition of non-being, is that it always induces self-reflection. Its power is strong enough to force us to penetrate the surface of personality and even to discover our common metaphysical structure.

The basis for insight through anxiety must therefore be the substratum of Being which can be made evident through a particular individual's experience of it as reflected in this state. Through this, of course, the possible elements of human nature are made clear and the variety of Being's human manifestations can even be discovered. But the metaphysical basis of severe psychological states can be made evident by self-reflection, if it is directed toward the elements of human nature which lie internal to the self. Thus self-reflection is also the origin of all the forms that structure the short story. It gives rise to all literary insights from its own modes of activity; i.e., from its ability to see beneath the surface of experience. Thereby it produces, in a metaphysical manner, the dramatic form by means of which whatever is to be known by literary insight is a product of that essentially metaphysical mode of creativity.

We are not concerned with the nature of human beings in their outer differentiations, because these are not connected with the element of human nature that gives us self-insight and self-reflection. We are concerned with literature as it reveals the metaphysical basis for a dramatic sense. In this instance self-reflection, since it makes dramatic form possible, thereby insists that the world of insight is either merely a psychological state produced by the internal dramatic grasp or that it is metaphysics as it is found in literature. That is to say, the existence of human beings is given structure by the insights of literature, because the metaphysical structure was first given to literature by the grasp of Being in insight. This mode of Being is revealed and given form primarily through literature. Artistic insight can now become metaphysically conscious structure and be sure of its basis in the immediately real.

The System of Psychological States of Being

There can be nothing more desirable to a philosopher than to be able to derive the scattered multiplicity of the situations which require ethical decision—as they appear in concrete life from a metaphysically based principle—and then to show how it is possible to unite everything in this way through a single literary grasp. Some philosophers have believed that those human beings who root themselves steadfastly in comparatively concrete situations actually lead the only completely collected lives; but this is only an *aggregate* of experience. Some other philosophers assert that only a few individuals, strong in the world's ways, can acquire such a concrete grasp upon themselves and upon life.

Our position is that a metaphysically grounded grasp is possible to any who can acquire the depth required for an internal dramatic participation, whether they are strong in the world's ways or not. This can constitute a comprehension of existence, and with it any individual can attain a psychological theory based on insight, whether his empirical success in the world is great or small. Writers are not usually society's pillars, but their understanding can still be strong.

We search in our common psychological experience for situations which do not rest upon particular aspects of the external circumstances of life. This can occur in a knowledge derived from any profound grasp of a dramatic presentation of life. It does not automatically provide meaning but is merely the occasion for the addition of meaningfulness. Such a literary search presupposes neither greater reflection nor deeper insight than to detect in a language the basis for the actual use of words which yields structure and thus collects metaphysical elements for a grammar of Being (in fact, both enterprises are very closely related). Such an undertaking has just this and no other real aim: to uncover Being; and we find that literature and drama restore this function to language, whereas ordinary use makes grammar dull in comparison with the writer's extraordinary use and the actor's unusual emphasis. Words come alive in these situations, and then they can become tools for metaphysical exploration—or vice versa.

But in order to discover such an existential directive for metaphysics, we need a deep and unusual enough process of self-reflection. It should be distinguished by the ability to cause us to see what was not before apparent in our own lives, by reducing the multiplicity of signs to a single direction and by leading us to basic structures. This kind of process of self-reflection is often present in literary construction. Here, then, the labors of the psychological explorations of the existentialists are ready at hand, though not yet quite free from defects. With this help, we can now work out a metaphysical foundation for psychological insight. Through that force of penetration, what was not accessible now can become so. These unexpected sources can yield an essential knowledge of human beings and of Being which is now made possible through certain basic self-reflections induced in literature.

Insight into the nature of the psychological states, which employs them as the metaphysical base for dramatic structure, actually never seems to have occurred to their first author, Kierkegaard. Yet without this insight (which immediately explains the derivation or origin of metaphysics) such experiences are quite useless and are only a depressing list of moods without explanation or definite potentialities for philosophical use. And this is how many have viewed the results of existentialism. Had modern philosophers ever conceived such a notion as that implied but not developed in Kierkegaard's work, doubtless the whole study of psychological investigation—which under the name of empiricism has for centuries held many a sound mind from deeper insight—would have reached us in quite another shape and would have enlightened all human self-reflection and led to positive construction. Instead, it was actually exhausted in obscure and vain psychological experimentation which rendered it unfit as a basis for true metaphysics.

This psychological ground for metaphysics indicates that the treatment of every psychological state by external observation is supposedly only sound theoretically, and it affords a direction or clue how and through what points of inquiry every metaphysical consideration must proceed to become concrete. For these Prolegomena concern the central functions of self-reflection within which even isolated situations can be penetrating and revealing. In like manner the source for ethical directives has at least been formulated, the soundness of which we can vouch for only by simultaneous metaphysical construction and empirical test. There is no doubt that the structure of any crisis in the human situation requires either self-reflection or extreme penetration to uncover its roots, insofar as it is to be of value metaphysically or ethically, and metaphysics can in this way be known concretely.

And this theory, like every other true one which might be founded on a revealing ethical crisis, shows its value in that it excludes all ordinary situations, and yet it makes significant the place of every literary and dramatic grasp of existence. These revealing stresses, which have been found intriguing for drama but have been ignored for metaphysics, are at once empirically grounded and yet revealing. Owing to this dual quality, they can enter into the formation of an ontology with a privilege and a claim to be among the basic structures able to produce a decisive self-reflection that is capable of structuring Being too. The connection between psychological states and possible modes of existence can be grasped and thus reveal the human situation itself.

Some literature, it is true, produces only romantic memories which merely lead to a comparison of situations already experienced and hence are of quite another nature and so of no use in the formulation of a metaphysics. By the theoretical foundation uncovered in the psychological state of crisis, metaphysics is saved from groundlessness, and certain psychological states can be made useful as a foundation for metaphysical construction. Because the existential insights into existence are of an entirely different nature and origin, the use made of them must take quite another form than the accumulation of empirical psychological data and experiment. This possible separation has not yet been fully explored in theoretical metaphysics, although Heidegger and phenomenology are a mild start. As a rule metaphysical structures have been all mixed up with the particular circumstances that produced the original self-reflection as though they were children of the same family. Such a confusion was unavoidable in the absence of a definite theory of existentially produced psychological insights into Being, and this alone can serve as an empirical basis for the construction of a meaningful metaphysics.[2]

Surveys, Conclusions, and Reconstruction

In his *Prolegomena* Kant set out to determine whether and how metaphysics is possible; and in the third part, after having considered pure mathematics and science of nature, he then drew his findings together in an attempt to answer the question of

2 At this point the original (though later completely revised) "translation" of Kant into existentialist concepts ended. What follows for the remainder of this chapter is a summary commentary based upon both the results of that first experimental translation and Kant's own conclusion to his *Prolegomena*. Part 2 will then move on independently of any parallel to Kant to begin to draw the preliminary metaphysical conclusions based on, or suggested by, this exploration.

metaphysics' future. In brief, a metaphysics of the structure of experience turns out to be possible for Kant, but a metaphysics of things in themselves is, on the same ground, rendered impossible. Metaphysics has seldom escaped this division since Kant first inaugurated the separation. Kant restricted metaphysics to subjective (although universal) application. What he did not see (and perhaps his explorations at that time could not be carried further) was that this path, when pursued far enough, could lead back to a grasp of Being's ultimate structure. Although this has been done in other ways (e.g., in Hegel's *Phenomenology*), in more recent times the existentialists have (although perhaps unintentionally) also provided another empirically grounded psychological exploration for just such a metaphysical "breakthrough."

Kant's goal is still not perfectly achieved on this basis, however. For in his own time he felt that metaphysics must be a science, which meant the construction of a necessary, single structure. Hegel thought it possible to produce such a single, though complicated and necessary, theory simply from the mind. Although owing certain inspirations to Hegel, the existentialists differ from him in that their psychological explorations reveal a basic uncertainty (i.e., possibility) and not a necessity to be at the heart of Being. Thus, the anxiety which is psychologically experienced is not a false impression to be banished by reason (à la Spinoza) but is actually a clue to Being's structure.

The experience of nonbeing produces the extreme psychological states upon which the existentialists dwell, so that their novelty is to discover nonbeing in tracing out an origin for their dread. Then, they use nonbeing as the basis upon which to understand Being, a reversal of the classical approach in vogue since Plato's *Sophist*. With nonbeing as the basis for establishing metaphysics, however, certainty and singularity must go. Metaphysics can now be based only on a variety of possibilities, or so Part 2 will go on to argue, since it takes its metaphysical starting point from this crucial conclusion.

Kant made the conditions for the possibility of experience the same source from which the laws of nature are to be derived. Since he focused on mathematics and physics as they were understood in his day, the result was a theory which is both necessary and singular. Setting aside the question whether mathematics and physics as they are today (i.e., involving choice as the only necessity) would themselves yield a contemporary metaphysics of different qualities, it is still true that the existentialists do focus on another (though certainly no less real) aspect of experience; e.g., anxiety and dread.

Metaphysics is here grounded in immediate experience, as Kant demanded, but the experience is such that, although it does lead to metaphysics, it is to a metaphysics of a radically different kind. The existentialists themselves were often in such strong revolt against the dialectically necessary metaphysics of Hegel that they used their psychological explorations of vital areas of experience to argue against Hegelian theories. In doing this they failed to see that, though their explorations did call Hegel into question, they might also found a new and more acceptable metaphysics on the same empirical base.

The existentialists opened new doors to an exciting and flexible metaphysics but they themselves were so caught up in rebellion that it remains for others to enter in by the path which they charted. Fearing Hegelian dialectic, they did not attempt the metaphysical construction which their psychological profundity had actually made possible. The "Interlude" in Kierkegaard's *Fragments* has within it the seeds for a radical reconstruction of metaphysics that would bring the era of historical investigation to an end in one stroke. Yet it remains for him an undeveloped "interlude," rather than a new theory of Being based upon his sensitivity to the psychological impact of nonbeing (see our Epilogue).

Kant had no way to break through to base any metaphysical theory on objects themselves. In extreme psychological states the existentialists have found a point of breakthrough. The resulting metaphysics, however, is of such different quality than Kant had expected that the constructive task was in their day never attempted, because it was never clearly seen. If metaphysics should still mean necessity and singularity of theory, the existentialists' empirical ground can never provide that. But they can provide an empirically grounded metaphysics of quite different qualities, one based on uncertainty, freedom, and choice as characteristic even of Being itself. Kierkegaard's most interesting paradox is one he never mentions or develops systematically: a radical psychology which discovers the centrality of nonbeing in every structure *vs.* a conservative and traditional God whose nature is never revised in the light of S. K.'s profound discoveries.

When Kant turned from the analysis of intuition to an exploration of judgments, he began on a line which might have brought him out differently had it been considered in itself. But he patterned his explanation of judgment after the universality and necessity which he claimed to find in intuition. The point in experience with which one starts often remains the touchstone of the whole structure. 'Judgment' might have become more flexible, but the pattern which he established in analyzing intuition prevailed. On the other hand, the existentialists begin, not with perception, but with emotional states. Their problem is not to escape this touchstone but to develop it fully into an acceptable metaphysics. Since the uncertainty which lies in the paradigm experience remains, no single metaphysics can possibly emerge—except perhaps what they did not see as possible; i.e., a meta-metaphysics which reflects on all possible metaphysics.

Kant bequeathed to every subsequent philosopher the problem of the a priori, so that metaphysics has hardly been able to move away from this question. 'Experience,' as Kant knew it, would not yield a metaphysics as Kant understood it. Therefore he and all metaphysicians who accept both perception as the starting point and necessity as the aim of metaphysics must face the issue of the a priori. On the other hand, if we follow the existentialists' focus on the extreme psychological experiences, we have here a type of 'experience' which can certainly ground a metaphysics against idle speculation. Yet we also get from this an interesting metaphysics which is quite different from that which Kant desired. The perplexing problem of the a priori need no longer dominate metaphysics, that is, if we change our perspective on experience (à la existentialist literature) and are contemporary enough to discover metaphysics in a new form.

The "synthetical" problem need plague such a new metaphysics no more, for that arises only because the analysis of perception, which Kant accepted from Hume, contained no such quality, and this required that the constructive aspect be discovered elsewhere. In the presentation of experience which can be found in the plays and novels of existentialism, the internal psychological explorations find no such radical discontinuities constitutive of experience. Instead, these experiences have such an impact and such a basic quality that in them all men are bound together in common ties. Inner suffering unites us as nothing else can. Original experience now is not disconnected, and so metaphysics' first problem is no longer synthesis. The connections which result here are flexible enough to make freedom the new metaphysical basis. Flexibility, not necessity, is its result.

Kant was certain that the categories which he discovered were all that there were or ever could be and that metaphysics required such exhaustiveness for its possibility. Hegel too believed in absolute comprehensiveness, so that when the existentialists challenged this with the doctrines of the 'moment', 'absurdity', and 'uncertainty', metaphysics itself seemed to fail. But if metaphysics can be true and yet partial, trustworthy without being exhaustive, acceptable without being the only possible theory—existentialism can give rise to metaphysics of this "nondogmatic" type. Kant, of course, achieved this exhaustive character for his categories by restricting their scope to experience as he had analyzed it. But if we do not demand such absolute certainty in our metaphysics, the fear of a lack of necessity need no longer drive us to restrict metaphysics' scope in the hope of eluding uncertainty. Now we are adrift on the sea whose ends we cannot fully establish, but a metaphysics geared to such a situation is fortunately once again possible. We may still learn, even when the modern and arrogant human demand for unquestioned certainty is abandoned.

Kant restrained his inquiry from dealing with things in themselves in the hope of achieving a scientific certainty through such a restriction. The existentialist psychology has broken through at points of stress to Being itself, but, as a consequence, it must rear a metaphysics that is a continuous inquiry and that is incapable of completion in an untouchable form. The existentialists have brought us closer to Being than Kant (this is our Copernican counterrevolution), but we have also discovered in Being the depths of its power and the basic uncertainty of our

momentary theoretical certainties. Kant was absolutely strict
with himself and would not allow what he had developed from
his corner of experience to be extended uncritically to things-in-
themselves. The ground which he had prepared for metaphysics
could not be used for its construction. A "metaphysics of
experience" then became possible, but not the hoped-for
ontology. If we find that the existentialist psychology is a path
that leads to Being in a way that perception never does, such a
ground may be transferred as a basis upon which Being itself can
now be understood.

For Kant, things-in-themselves surely existed as the objects
which metaphysics traditionally had sought, but they could not
be reached via the avenue that he had chosen to enter. The only
route open was to examine experience for its structure, and this
enterprise has absorbed several generations of philosophers since.
The self, of course, was the only certain center here, and hence
metaphysics has been committed to a sustained egocentricity
almost without relief. The existentialists' concentration upon the
self is, it is true, almost as totally absorbing and at times almost
as overpowering as its romantic counterpart. But the radical
elements which the existentialists discovered (e.g., in the extreme
psychological states that they chose morbidly to dwell upon)
actually carried them through. Feeling the power of nonbeing
breaking through the walls of the psyche, they followed this new
route from nonbeing to Being. In this instance, an extreme
concentration on the self led us away from it, or through it, to
the power of Being and nonbeing discovered as breaking in upon
the self. Similarly, the religious consciousness begins with
extreme self-concentration, but, if it is successful, it then moves
beyond this preoccupation.

In the third part of his *Prolegomena* Kant had to end by
restricting metaphysics to pure rational concepts which can never
appear in experience, thus separating metaphysics from the
experience which he had hoped would ground it. The experience
that the existentialists emphasize is not so circumscribed, and it
actually proves to be explained more by what confronts the self
than by the self's own structure, as was the case with Kant.
Concentrating on these disrupting psychic states (e.g., dread)
actually opened up an area to the self other than its own

structure. Nonbeing was here and could thus be the route to Being, but only of course to a metaphysics which was of a quite different variety. Having a traditional view of metaphysics, the existentialists did not see what they had in fact opened up, and consequently they did not begin the new constructive task themselves. That is an uncompleted task for our generation to take up.

Reason ended by being dissatisfied with the empirical restrictions which Kant had developed for it, so that even Kant was not content with his own result in the first *Critique*. The extended critical analysis of sense experience was not as fruitful for metaphysics as he had hoped. Many will not follow Kant from sense experience on to the other two *Critiques,* but these do indicate Kant's own awareness that other kinds of experience might yield different results for metaphysics. Indeed, this is very true of the two later *Critiques,* but Kant had a distaste for psychology, so that the area of experience which the existentialists were later to stress was by him left unexplored. Hegel developed one side of this virgin area, i.e., the rational side; but the more radical portion was uncovered by existentialism, although the shock effect of this strong material is so great that its metaphysical possibilities remained unexplored until recently.

Of course, reason cannot find here the completeness which to Kant it seemed to demand. A metaphysics based upon uncertainty and chance is on the whole a new idea (which we will begin to explore in part 2) , although others in our age (e.g., Whitehead) have already moved in that direction. The soul as substance remained for Kant beyond all possible experience, but that was 'experience' as sense experience and judgment and not the unsettling 'experience' of a severe emotional reaction. This, of course, will reveal a soul different in nature than Kant conceived; he could not have been expected to find such a kind of radical entity, since it never occurred to him to look for it. Reason was left with antinomies by Kant until some radically new material could move it from its fixed course. The impact of the 'absurd' is just the kind of experience mhich is able to break the balance of the antinomies and to end by reforming radically the notion of metaphysics itself.

Kant concludes that we cannot, following his critical method carefully, assert that our experience is the only mode of knowing things. For him, ethical and aesthetical modes are two alternatives. Now the issue is whether the existentialists have, intentionally or unintentionally, added a third and metaphysically more important mode: literary and psychological moods in boundary situations. Kant knows that experience cannot satisfy reason fully, but he cannot himself seem to break through the rigid walls which he erected that separate experience from our direct knowledge of things themselves. Can a psychological crisis-situation, when dramatically presented in isolated instances, achieve this breakthrough? This is our contemporary metaphysical hope. Kant sought an identity of modes which his starting point in experience could not allow him to achieve, since it was based on a separation which he could not overcome. Metaphysics is left as an actual disposition but not as a constructive enterprise when Kant is through.

Kant ends his *Prolegomena* indicating that the standard upon which to judge metaphysical construction has not yet been found. What he began his *Prolegomena* to accomplish, his own procedures prevented him from accomplishing, yet not in such a way as to dispel the hope or to rule out the possibility. The analysis of pure reason made metaphysics even more necessary as the only area where the contradictions of experience might be resolved. Beginning with existence's absurdity when taken in itself, the existentialists have found, in their exploration of the psychological impact of nonbeing, a reflection of metaphysics' object. But like traditional negative theology, the best approach to Being is the *via negativa,* in this instance the reflection of nonbeing in negative psychological moods. Here a contemporary but radically transformed metaphysics can begin.

Part Two

*The Beginning of a
New Metaphysics*

5

The Derivation of
Abstract Knowledge

The Abstract and the Concrete

If it were conscious, this small chapter should fear for its life, since it attempts to accomplish what has perplexed philosophy from its origin: the union between abstract thought and concrete experience. Yet at least to attempt something like this is crucial to the thesis of this brief Prolegomenon. If metaphysics has been suspect because it did not seem to have any firm empirical ground by which it could be tested, and if we claim to have found in existential psychology and literature just such a ground, we should at least be able to begin to show how a metaphysical view can be derived directly from such a source. It is true that we have never claimed in this essay to be presenting a complete metaphysics or a full systematic theology. To do that is important, according to the thesis of this prolegomenon, but it is also a life's work, or perhaps even an effort requiring more lives than one.

Yet if a promise is not idle, at least a direction must be pointed out and a beginning made. In the following chapters we will explore the kind of metaphysics which seems to be dictated by part 1. If the reader will take note, there are many times in the course of the following considerations where reference will be made to the material of part 1 to show how, in a specific instance, it seems to lead to one metaphysical conclusion rather than to some alternative one. In that sense, the answer to the question raised by this particular chapter is to be found spread throughout the whole of the essay, but especially in part 2. Still, a question which perennially is so important and which is so central to the thesis of this prolegomenon also needs some direct treatment, and that is the task to which this chapter turns. To deal adequately with such an issue, of course, requires much more than a brief chapter, but then this is neither primarily an inquiry into theory of knowledge nor a completed metaphysics. Thus, this question will be dealt with as a point of prolegomena too.

In part 1 we discussed the concrete material produced by the existentialists and its implications. In the following chapters of part 2, we are for the most part engaged in metaphysical exploration which primarily is of an abstract quality. In what way, then, are parts 1 and 2 related? How are the abstract theses (speculations) to be connected to the concrete psychological explorations and to the literary material? Just to do metaphysics, however entertaining or instructive it may be, does not of itself prove our thesis—i.e., that this abstract metaphysics is grounded and comes from the concrete existential experienced as outlined in part 1. Yet, the most important point to note here is that it was never claimed that one and only one metaphysical view would necessarily follow from the existentialist prolegomena and establish itself with universal validity so as to exclude all other theories of Being. In fact, the opposite is the case. From these existentialist prolegomena we learn that our conception of metaphysics must itself first be changed.

Metaphysics can remain abstract and speculative and be filled for the most part with universalizable statements, but now no theoretical analysis of Being and nonbeing can establish itself as necessarily authoritative. Freedom and contingency are the chief themes of existentialist psychology and drama, and a metaphysics which draws on those empirical sources should reflect these same qualities in itself. Still, not every metaphysical view which meets these standards can be accepted. There perhaps are necessary conditions for a new metaphysics (i.e., contingency and freedom), but certainly these are not in themselves sufficient criteria on which to build—and to ground—an existentialist-derived description of the structure of Being. In the strictest sense, no final set of rules governing this derivation can be set down. As metaphysical questions are raised and responses are given in the form of new theories, the reader will simply have to "judge for himself" whether or not the position taken and the modifications made in traditional views seem in fact to have come from and to have been inspired by an existential empirical base.

The Elements of Metaphysics

This, of course, brings us to the problem of what materials go into a new metaphysics and how new insights are actually formed.[1] It might seem that one simply takes contemporary materials—e.g., those distilled in part 1—and out of these shapes new doctrines on Being and nonbeing. Such is not the case with metaphysics, and, if it were, no new doctrine would arise simply from either the existentialist psychological explorations or from literary activity alone. Being is not such, and our minds are not so related to it, that this is a possible approach to metaphysics. What actually takes place (it is our thesis) is something more like what the reader will observe in the following chapters. Certain traditional or contemporary theories present themselves in print, and, on a purely abstract and logical basis, there is not much ground to deny either that 'Being is one' or that 'Being is many'.

If an existentialist prolegomenon is really to be very helpful to us in a time of metaphysical and theological crisis, it cannot simply allow all speculations equally to be true. Rather, it must serve as a guide to the aspiring twentieth-century metaphysician. If it does not lead him firmly to one and only one metaphysics, at least it must give him the *concrete ground* upon which to decide to accept, reject, or modify some given *abstract formulation*. And how can such a principle of existential guidance be observed in operation as the construction of a metaphysics is begun? The answer is perhaps most immediately clear in chapter 6. Few concepts could be said to be more crucial to the history of both

1 For a more complete exploration of this problem see my *The Problems of Metaphysics* (San Francisco: Chandler Publishing Co., 1969).

metaphysics and theology than 'nothingness' and 'time'. Existentialist literature and psychology seem to raise these concepts to
prominence. This is done, not simply abstractly, but in terms
of immediate ethical and psychological significance in the life of
an individual.

Without rehearsing in advance the argument of the next
chapter, it seems that existentialism has not only provided an
empirical ground for the treatment of these classical abstract
problems, but it has, in the material which it presents, actually
given us guidance for revising these concepts in important ways.
As we come to new views on nothingness and time, we also see
Being structured in new ways, and this is nothing more nor less
than the traditional aim of metaphysics. Whether I have worked
out properly the new views on nothingness and time, and with
them have begun a correct revision of the structures of Being, the
reader will have to appraise. But such a question must be
separated sharply from the issue of this chapter; that is, whether
in fact it is the existentialist's concrete materials which guide the
author in this theoretical reconstruction of metaphysics, as is the
claim. The illustration of how the elements are derived to form a
new metaphysics is more clear in chapter 6, but how the elements
of chapter 7 are connected to existentialism, or how they can
begin a new metaphysics, is admittedly more difficult to
see.

As the opening section of chapter 7 will point out,
Wittgenstein has launched a kind of revival of metaphysics,
although in his own view it is probably neither connected to the
existentialist explorations nor intended as a conventional
metaphysical theory. But consider a metaphysical theory such as
Wittgenstein presents in the *Tractatus*. Unless one simply
dogmatically affirms it as the truth, on what grounds may a man
either modify some statements or oppose them with formulations
of his own? The followers of Wittgenstein undoubtedly have one
answer to this problem, but our aim is to illustrate the
existentialist beginning of a metaphysics at this point. That is,
one becomes aware as he reads the abstract descriptions of the
Tractatus that the world cannot be as it is described there and
the existentialist descriptions of experience still be true at the
same time. Existentialist psychology simply does not seem to fit
into a world such as Wittgenstein outlined.

Our project is not to consider either how Wittgenstein himself developed his views or how he changed his mind, but rather to ask how the existentialist prolegomen gives us a concrete basis to form a new view in opposition to Wittgenstein's. It probably is true that, simply by spinning off abstract ideas, one might not come to a kind of metaphysics of Being's structure that would fit the existentialist material. Yet, the fact that this can come about if we apply the existentialist concrete data to the admittedly abstract structure of Wittgenstein both tells us something about what elements must go together to form a useful metaphysics and gives us an insight into how an existentially based metaphysics can be started. The results of this exploration are open for inspection in chapter 7.

From any given concrete material we may not be able to form either an abstract statement which expresses it properly in theory or one which clearly connects the abstract formula to that concrete set of experiences. When propositions about the structure of the world and about Being in general are presented (e.g., Wittgenstein's *Tractatus*), however, one who has accepted the existentialist prolegomena may be able to begin a metaphysics by reacting against these given abstractions. His concrete material may not in itself tell him what he ought to believe abstractly, but it may give him the needed grounds upon which to know what to reject. And by this *via negativa* more acceptable abstractions may be formed which are more representative of the experience which they claim as their base. The revised metaphysical view to be seen in chapter 7 is not, therefore, somehow validated in itself. It does, however, illustrate how existentialist materials can be made to operate on existing elements of metaphysical theory to produce a view of Being through a negative reaction; i.e., one which more nearly accords with experience as the existentialists describe it.

Metaphysics and Theological Materials

As one beginning for a new metaphysics, the concluding chapter (8) may present to the reader an even more difficult problem as far as discerning the relationship of the existentialist prolegomena (part 1) to the abstract extensions (part 2) is concerned. In that chapter, no preexisting metaphysical system (such as Wittgenstein's) was encountered in reaction to which existentialist materials could provide a ground for revision—i.e., an alteration which ultimately leads to a new view. Yet if there is to be a new metaphysics, there must also be a new metaphysician. What kind of person will write the existentialist metaphysics? If the existentialists are right, their description of man is not merely of some few or of some peculiar state. Rather, it is the analysis of a special condition which in fact leads to and defines the essence of human existence. Nevertheless, if all men who understand their condition are, or should be, metaphysicians of the same general type, it still might be that God would differ from man in this respect. This is what the concluding chapter attempts to point out.

Classical metaphysics has been very closely associated with theology. It is as true to say that many theologians have rejected a traditional God, because he is too much like classical metaphysical concepts, as it is to say that many have rejected metaphysics itself (including some existentialists) because it seemed to be too closely connected with a view of God's nature which they could no longer accept. At least in this way a revival of metaphysics involves theology, and any successful new metaphysical base will have wide implications for contemporary theology, which now appears to be almost Godless. We must see man's metaphysical role anew, but it is also true that God's role is involved here too. A full-scale description of such an implied new conception of God cannot be given, nor can all its implications for a wide variety of theological problems be worked out. Yet, as a beginning, some contrast between the roles which God and man play in a contemporary metaphysics may be an illuminating starting point for both enterprises.

If the existential materials are to form the base, and if existing metaphysical schemes such as Wittgenstein's are to provide the occasion for accomplishing a revision, it might be that an application to theology is the best (and perhaps the traditional) testing ground on which to see what a new metaphysics involves and how it "works." Whether the reader will find the sketch given of God *vs.* man convincing or not (see chapter 8), it still may be that he can examine two things there: (1) how the existentialist materials in fact lead to a revision in the conception of and the doctrines in metaphysics, and (2) the implications in a revised metaphysics for the development of new views in another field (theology). If this is one testing ground for a metaphysical view, then as the ending indicates, ethics is another. A somewhat different view of God's nature will develop, and the effect of the existentialist base may perhaps be better appraised for its metaphysical fruitfulness (or for its faults) by observing its effects in one or another of these areas.

An important function of metaphysics is also illustrated here in chapter 8. In spite of the controversy which rages over the very possibility of metaphysics itself, it still may be true that, without its instrumentation, there are important areas which will remain unstructured and thus unclear to us. This is not the place to take up such a serious question in detail, but it just might be that the failure in our own day to conceive of God with any reality can actually be traced back to the decline of metaphysics. If God does not appear as a concrete object, some other context needs to be provided if we are to be able to structure a view of the divine nature which has any contemporary reality. One way, then, to test the beginnings of the proposed new metaphysics is to see what kind of God it is able to conceive of. The success of this experiment the reader can inspect in chapter 8. If it is true that Kierkegaard did not reconstruct his view of the divine nature on the basis of his existentialist discoveries, perhaps the decline in philosophical theology which we have experienced since his time simply indicates that this is a metaphysical revision which is already long overdue.

How Is God Known?

Is God a matter of direct experience? From what has just been said, it would not seem to be so. And yet we have also indicated that the existentialist materials give us some concrete data with which to fill in an abstract description. Therefore, though God is not experienced directly, it must still be that in the existentialist account some indirect contact can be found. Many have explored this possibility (e.g., Tillich) and nothing guarantees that one unified view of God will emerge from all these accounts. Nevertheless, it is theologically very important for the existentialist material to make possible a new experience of encounter with the divine nature, if only by indirection. Kierkegaard's notion in the *Fragments* that all being is characterized by suffering is important here, for example. A more classical God was not capable of accepting such a condition, but on a basis extended beyond Kierkegaard's, God might be experienced in the crisis of suffering and in all the modifications on existent being which this involves.

To work out the detail is both a complicated and a long process, but the structure of a kind of God who might be experienced in this way is traced in these last chapters. Whatever other avenues to God religion may have (e.g., faith), it is not the function of these prolegomena and beginnings to inquire into them. Given traditional views and metaphysically structured issues, our question is what revisions may be worked out in a technical doctrine of the divine nature. Using the existentialist materials as a basis for reaction and new insight, what kind of revised view of God might be produced? In the brief results exhibited in the following chapters, the reader should be able to trace the view of God which is adopted back to the kind of experience which the existentialists stress. If the existentialists have uncovered an experience which lets Being be described in a different way, we should also be able to trace a new idea of God back to that same source.

For instance, nonbeing has usually been given a very minor role in the divine nature. Now, existentialism insists that it is a key to all metaphysical interpretation, and this leads us to reevaluate its importance in God's being and to assign it a major role. Contingency has usually been excluded from the divine nature, but the existentialist stress upon its fundamental importance gives us new reason to reexamine its possible inclusion in God's nature too. It is not that either nonbeing or contingency were not known before. They certainly were, and in describing God's nature they were rejected as incompatible with the perfection necessary for his role as a creator. What has changed is that the existentialist description reveals these qualities to be so deeply embedded in the structure of Being itself that it is no longer possible to accept them as simply minor indications of man's weakness. Instead, we must now consider whether or not they are pervasive structures, so fundamental to all beings and to Being that a new appraisal must be made of their possible source in God himself.

Or further, consider God's action and intention at creation. It has usually been taken for granted that God's nature led him to one form of creation at a fixed point. We now find contingency and decision to be at the very center of existence. This certainly suggests to us that we might develop a view of God in which his own choices are contingent, open to alternatives and dependent upon the movement of the divine will in decision. In certain ways this brings the divine life closer to the human mode of existence, but that parallel is subject to certain qualifications, and this is what the last chapter attempts to explore. That God should be unmoved, as he has sometimes been described, and the existentialist awareness of being still be so severe, is a paradox which may be lessened by beginning a revision of the divine nature so that the existentialist psychology does not seem so far removed from God's nature itself.

The Existential Sources

The view of Being to be suggested in the following chapters is that it is an absolutely infinite set of possibilities. In the strictest sense, no such theory is "derived" from the existentialist analysis. Yet, in considering the view of the world which one gets in existentialist literature (e.g., the famous dictum that existence precedes essence), it is clear that ours is not a world of strict necessity, that many alternatives are open, and that man shapes the resulting structure through his own decisive power, or the lack of it. The view of the nature of Being offered here is intended at least to be in harmony with this account, whereas, for example, Spinoza's 'Substance' certainly would not support such a view as reflecting the real nature of things.

In a sense, Being's structure has been made visible in the existentialist account, but neither directly nor fully. An abstract structure can assist in this process by describing Being's structure more directly so that it may become more clear what basic structure was discerned by the existential analysis—even when this is still clothed in its psychological explorations and literary presentations. Perhaps central to the existentialist claim is the importance of the encounter with nothingness. If this is so important to human nature, it should also be central to reality, and so any metaphysics which builds on this ground should (as will be suggested here) use nothingness and nonbeing as its key for the interpretation of Being. Existentialism clearly suggests such a metaphysical approach. It is true that the result of following this suggestion cannot in the nature of the case lead to one and only one abstract doctrine, but at least we can require that any abstract metaphysics exhibit its use of these concrete materials, and this should be true of the chapters which follow.

For example, on pages 138 and 141 in the next chapter, we will try to explain how this description of our behavior requires that Being contain nonbeing. Or again, contingency and possibility as our major metaphysical problems will be traced to their existential ground in the analysis of nothingness and time. Then, on page 179, it is suggested that "existential immediacy" can help us assess which abstract theory (however elegant it is in itself) actually comes closest to reality as it is experienced (on this account). Thus, any metaphysical theory must be requested to contain internally an account of its assessment of its own degree of probability. In these ways, then, the existentialist base does not demand a certain metaphysics, but it does shape up a set of criteria both for the construction and the assessment of contemporary metaphysics. Both of these processes are begun in the remaining three chapters.

The concept of a "philosophical psychology," of course, is our key here, as we discussed in chapter 3. Undoubtedly this needs even further exploration and refinement than a prolegomenon alone can yield, but the argument does depend upon rendering psychological terms suitable for philosophical construction. For instance, we all experience time, and the existentialists have described vividly our experience of nothingness. If the psychological impact of this experience can be used as a philosophical tool (see the next chapter), this will tend to support the primacy of contingency in Being, since here the experience seems to be that there is no absolute reason for anything to be as it is. The experience of such contingency in the encounter with nothingness is psychologically upsetting, but our question is whether it is also metaphysically revealing. *The existential sources for metaphysics will validate themselves if the abstract relations drawn from them form a rational explanation for the psychological experience described.*

Existential Methods and Metaphysical Description

The reader who continues on to the remaining chapters and attempts to discover how the following abstract descriptions of reality are based on or are derived from the preceding existentialist insight may notice that it is not clear whether God or Being is to be considered ultimate. Although it is far from true in every account given, here it may be assumed that both terms refer to the same first principle. A metaphysics need not lead to a theology, but in this instance the principle of Being itself, as its description is worked out, turns out to have the central attributes also required of a creator God. The existentialist insight does not reveal a ground in Being of the more classical type, e.g., necessity and completion. But it does reveal a kind of view of Being which, when extended, actually can lead to a concept of God that is much more personal in its description as it is encountered. Kierkegaard did not find his God to be like this, it is true, but then he did not extend his psychological explorations into a metaphysics or a theology.

In the opening sections of this chapter a little has already been said about how, in the succeeding three chapters, the speculative statements were arrived at. For each statement the avenue from the existential methods to the metaphysical description is different, and this seems to indicate a basic variability in the way in which the abstract statements can be derived from and related to these existentialist prolegomena. In any case, it seems that other materials must be added too. Even a successful prolegomenon cannot turn itself into a completed metaphysics unless that suggestive material is placed in some other already existing context. Then, as the existentialists' suggestions shape a reaction to and a revision of the materials encountered (whether of God or of Wittgenstein), we can see how a metaphysical description is guided and tends to take place on the basis of such a method.

It is certainly true, then, that metaphysical views other than the one begun here can arise and claim the same existential origin. We cannot be guaranteed a single set of abstract propositions, but at least we have a common source which (1) serves as a point of reference; (2) guides the modification of existing views by reacting on them; and (3), which perhaps is most important, is fruitful and suggestive enough to break up old patterns of thought and to produce new insight through a fresh approach. That is not all we require of a metaphysics; forming the detail of a systematic view is a very complex matter. But still, that is a great deal of fresh impulse, plus a novel context and a point of reference, to derive from one prolegomenon.

Our question is, "How is metaphysical knowledge possible," and our hope has been to be able to find an empirical ground for an answer in the existentialist literature. Actually, the reader of these prolegomena will find two answers to this question (part 1 and part 2). In part 1 we explored the existentialist materials as a ground for an answer to Kant. Now in part 2 we move on to certain abstract speculations about the nature of things. An observant reader will, we hope, take note of the points where at least certain of the views proposed in the next chapters are suggested by the existentialist prolegomena. It is hoped that all the speculations which follow can be traced to the same source. But given the nature of metaphysics, inasmuch as it requires previous views as its material, an ideal like that could not be correct. It probably is not true that no one else has yet made this same attempt. The efforts of Sartre and Heidegger, for example, are clearly pointed to in the next chapter. Nevertheless, in what follows it is hoped that the reader can observe how the preceding material helped to shape and to ground these additional—and we hope new—speculations.

6

The Problems of Metaphysics: Nothingness and Time

Change and Continuity in Metaphysics

If it is true that the existentialists have succeeded where Kant failed and that they have established a ground upon which metaphysical construction can take place, is it true that metaphysical problems always remain the same? Kant hoped for a foundation for metaphysics and could not find it in his *Critique of Pure Reason.* The existentialists, although often antimetaphysical in the Hegelian sense, have actually provided an empirical ground in their psychology and literature but perhaps without explicitly intending to. Yet are the metaphysical problems with which we can now deal constructively exactly the same ones which Kant wanted to answer, or do the problems of metaphysics themselves change as well as our ability to answer them? Is part of the success of the existentialists due to the fact that they have reformulated the questions themselves, not just that they have now found a way to deal with previously unanswerable questions? In what sense do metaphysical questions change, and in what sense is continuity with past inquiry maintained?

Certainly Being itself, considered as the absolutely infinite set of possibles, does not change. It is now and ever shall be what it is, without addition or subtraction. The actualization of certain sets of possibles, however, is what makes one age different from another, although whatever is discovered and actualized remains a part of Being and in that sense is subject to its unchanging structure too. Our apprehension of Being, of course, can change. This is particularly true of the way in which we set this down in written form.

Philosophy has no way of being transmitted except via the written and the spoken word, so that our metaphysical foundations are subject to as much change as there are different ways of saying things. The variety and flexibility of our language medium varies the form in which metaphysical problems are given, and sometimes increases, sometimes decreases, our insight into Being's structure. A "new way" may only be a new way of saying things, of opening insight through a new approach. One way of phrasing a problem may seem particularly unfruitful, while another way may open it to new exploration. Only the dogma that there is only one way to express a problem needs to be resisted as being metaphysically stifling.

Old metaphysics may be brought back to life; it may once more provide a means to understand Being. That is, it will if enough study is put into it, so that it can again become a usable verbal vehicle. Now its terms work again to provide a structure that will support understanding. Of course, novelty attracts energy more easily, so that there is usually more desire to push ahead to new formulas than to revive old ones, although the mastery of an old structure is often the only way to learn how a new one can be built.

Could men escape the necessity to use words as an intermediary, could we look directly at Being's structure as we do the pattern of the empirical world, we might escape constant change in the formulation of metaphysical theory. But only the empirical sense world is given to our sight; and, since metaphysical structure is never identical with this, we must always use techniques of indirection. This means that the words of any theory are not the structures themselves, and thus they can never escape change as we work with them. We try constantly to shape them to do the impossible, i.e., to express Being directly and perfectly.

By expressing our theories in verbal form, we do give them a certain fixed continuity which allows them to be transmitted, and this testifies to the factual and unalterable nature of the objects which the written formulas comment upon. Yet such verbal forms are subject to constant reinterpretation by being remolded. By interpreting the written word new interpretations constantly arise. Difficulties call forth renewed theoretical attempts as they are encountered. And yet, our only factual data are not sense impressions. Psychological experience is equally immediate, even though not as visible, which is what the existentialists have revealed via their psychology and their literature.

This being so, metaphysics can have an empirical anchor. Its theories cannot escape the constant flow which words by nature are subject to, but we at least have an abundance of concrete material to use as a base for our contemporary formulations of the constant metaphysical problems. We can understand and control the change in our theoretical foundations about Being even if it is not within our power to prevent all change in theory. We have a new context, a new background, which we have good reason to hope may induce stability into our verbal metaphysical structures; i.e., give a fixed point of reference to our terms.

What Metaphysical Questions Can Now Be Asked?

If the metaphysical structure of Being remains constant, though the actual structure and the verbal formulations about it may vary, in any age we must determine what questions may profitably be asked. Kant had a certain theoretical view of metaphysics, but by forming his questions as he did, he could not find a substantial base upon which to answer them. If in retrospect we now find a base for metaphysical inquiry in the explorations of the existentialists, it is also true that the metaphysical questions themselves will have changed at least slightly. We do now have a new entry into traditional metaphysics, but only with an altered form of the question. Radical novelty in formulation is not commensurate with the constant metaphysical structure of the infinite extent of Being's possible entities, but a new ground for inquiry alters the form of the question asked, just as actualization in a concrete configuration can alter the structure of the possibles in that sense.

That we should ask about the form of contemporary metaphysical questions is particularly appropriate where Sartre and Heidegger are involved. (Kierkegaard's "new material" will be considered in the Epilogue; the first of the existentialists shall be the last.) Both Sartre and Heidegger give at least some stress to questioning (and to listening too) as fundamental to man's being and as insightful into Being in general. What is it about the act of questioning and its basic place in our being which in itself can give us a ground for metaphysical inquiry? The uncertainty involved in questioning is easily discovered, and perhaps it is easier to see here why literature can have philosophical relevance, since drama discloses man's uncertainty in a graphic manner and thus gives us evidence for the centrality which questioning has. Psychological exploration and the technical use of emotional terms (e.g., 'dread', 'care') again set down a concrete base that makes uncertainty and questioning a natural mode. Questioning is here revealed to be, not a temporary or a provisional state, but a basic structure of our being which always remains. This discovered fact defines our relation to Being, and it is able to give us an insight into Being itself.

Decision—and the necessity for it—is perhaps the main theme emerging from existentialist psychology and literature. Without the recovery of a sense of the centrality of decision in man's being, no existentialist revival of metaphysics would be possible. Questioning has been revealed as a necessity, not merely as a sign of lack of information, and, this now being the only absolute, the hold of necessity on metaphysics is removed. The questioning of man, his uncertainty, and the demand for decision as the only way out and as the single necessity raise metaphysical questions as probabilities, no longer as a search for unconditional certainties. All actual structure depends upon some decision, either God's or man's (see chapter 8 for an elaboration of this point) . Metaphysical questions need no longer seek certainty and necessity. Instead, probability is sufficient, and their aim is to uncover a basis for decision in the face of the precariousness of existence. Metaphysical questions of this type find a natural ground in depth psychology and literary style, and this the existentialists have provided.

How do existentialist literature and psychological exploration establish such metaphysical questions as 'empirical'? In the first place, the experiences upon which they focus are certainly immediate and, they argue, universal to all men, even if all men do not experience them as graphically or as forcefully as the existentialists indicate. Existentialist situations have emotional force, and this may be what is required to open metaphysical structure to view and to make such questions meaningful by grounding them in the emotional life. Such a grounding might not seem rationally acceptable to a necessitarian and to a deterministically oriented metaphysics. But if decision is fundamental in the world's structure and if questioning is merely man's reflection of this, then emotion is not philosophically immaterial and it can be accepted as empirical data. The questions of metaphysics themselves, however, change when placed upon such a base. This may be one reason why many existentialists have not recognized their work as an existentialist prolegomenon to a contemporary metaphysics, because by 'metaphysics' they understood an old way of phrasing the questions.

What this chapter wants to ask, in this light, is how 'nothingness' and 'time' emerge as the chief metaphysical problems of our era; how these questions are still traditional and yet in some sense novel; and—most of all—how each is grounded in some immediate psychological experience or explored in a literary mode. Have the existentialists given empirical ground for a metaphysics of 'nothingness' and 'time', and if so, how does this alter the conception of metaphysics, its task, and its problems? How can we say that 'nothingness' and 'time' are the central metaphysical problems for which the existentialists have provided a prolegomena which at once satisfies Kant's demand but at the same time alters our conception of metaphysics and its questions? The irony of philosophy's history is embodied here: we can answer a traditional question, previously unanswered, only by altering the form of the question. Thus, if this is true, the only dogmatism that is dangerous to philosophy is the one which thinks its form of the question the only possible one.

Being and its structure are not self-evident. That is our most important conclusion. Were they, this constant reformulation might not be necessary. Abstract structure is not Being itself, and yet the strange fact is that it can make Being's structure visible. We create a theoretical framework by using concepts previously found meaningful. As this verbal and mental structure is crystalized, it enables the mind to grasp what it cannot see directly. Kant, of course, did not trust this, and it is true that many speculative structures seem to be only internally meaningful. If our emotional and dramatic life are irrelevant, we are left with ungrounded pure reason. But if psychology and literature actually reveal Being's structure, we can have an empirical base for our speculative structure.

As will be developed later (see chapter 8), metaphysics does require that human nature transcend itself. Kant may be right—that pure reason can do this but that in doing so it cannot be trusted. What can force man's transcendence of the immediate and yet still retain some empirical guide? The encounter with 'nothingness' seems to do this, just as an analysis of 'time' necessitates a movement away from the present and an extension to both past and future. God does this by his nature and through his very being, so that, curiously, it is the experience of nothingness (not of immediate being) which forces man to transcend himself and to become like God, in the sense of understanding via theoretical structure. The dread which can be induced by an experience of the nothingness present in his being may actually force man away from immediacy, and it can enable him to transcend his limitation to the present moment. Without the shock of the experience of nonbeing in one's own nature, neither speculative construction would be possible nor could any experience be of sufficient depth and solidity to ground it.

Man transcends time via the encounter with negativity, and God transcends time by virtue of his being, so that it is the negative elements in our structure which make human metaphysics possible. The ancient *via negativa* was much used as the medieval way to God. Now the modern avenue to metaphysics proves to be the experience of the negative modes within our own being. Just as many have felt that God is knowable only by indirection, so the structures of Being prove not to be immediately accessible but to come light only in the experience of negativity.

Why then, if this path is open to us, is there no accepted modern metaphysics? Is it that its origin in uncertainty means that it must be a contingent and not a necessary truth, and that we are not accustomed to associate such uncertainty with metaphysics? With nonbeing as primary in experience, certainty and singularity of theory become impossible; and the prime problems of metaphysics now become possibility and contingency. 'Nothingness' and 'time', when they are central, remove a priori knowledge as our dominant problem. When we once demanded certainty and necessity, a priori knowledge seemed to be the only way. With contingency and possibility as our problems, experience can provide their immediate ground in nothingness and time. That is the theme of this chapter, and the first extension of the *Prolegomena* (part 1) into a new metaphysics (part 2).

Sartre and Nothingness

The classical texts for our modern empirical metaphysics are found in Sartre's *Being and Nothingness*,[1] primarily in part 1, chapter 1, "The Origin of Negation." Questioning is again the basic human phenomenon which forms our context, for it is in tracing out the questioning situation that nothingness is discovered. For the being who questions is aware that there must exist for him the permanent objective possibility of a negative reply to every question (p. 5). For a question to be meaningful it must be possible for the answer to be negative, and it must also spring from a lack within the questioner. An understanding of

1 All page references in this section are to that volume. J. P. Sartre, *Being and Nothingness*, trans. Hazel Barnes (New York: Philosophical Library, 1956).

questioning reveals it to be a bridge between two nonbeings: the nonbeing of knowledge in man and the possibility of nonbeing outside of man in the object of his question. Questioning reveals nonbeing outside us and within us, and this uncovers the uncertainty of Being's structure that serves as a basis for a new metaphysics without certainty and necessity. Questioning, since it is essential to man's being, reveals nonbeing to be a part of what is most real.

How is it possible for negativity to exist or for men to take negative attitudes? We ask this in the Kantian form of necessary presuppositions: What must be true if negativity exists? Sartre answers: The necessary condition for our saying *not* is that nonbeing be a perpetual presence in us and outside of us (p. 11). 'Anguish' is the sign of our discovery of this situation, for it is a psychological response to the recognition of a painful fact about the structure of being (p. 18). It is "painful" because the human self, not having God's infinite power, grasps for necessity and certainty and finds, to its dismay, that negativity and nothingness are neither merely accidental nor temporary phenomena but instead are permanent features of the structure of Being itself. Negation as a phenomenon refers us back to nothingness in Being as its origin and foundation. Our psychological experience and our literary portrayal indicate that our being is always in question; but this, we discover, in turn opens to our view the fact that Nothingness is a central feature within Being itself.

By our questions we introduce a negative element into our own being in a way that no other form of existence can. Water does not stop its flow by questioning itself, but man does. The negative element we introduce into the world by questioning would not be possible if it were not actually a reflection of the nonbeing within Being. We must hold the process up to view in order to question it, and in doing so we step outside it; yet by this disengagement we threaten to bring the process itself to a halt and never to take it up again. Hamlet questions and does not act.

For this to be possible, Being must be such that man may disengage himself. He may freeze to inactivity in some vacant part of Being and no longer move in the regular causal structures. It is in nonbeing that man must exist when he questions. He is not that which he questions, but this at once enables man both to transcend Being and to be lost in its negative side. Questioning is our power and our danger—that is, if we do not soon move back from nothingness to some form of Being. The anguish present in the experience of the emptiness found within Being is the empirical ground for a new metaphysics of contingency.

Our questions can modify the structure of Being (p. 84). This is our power and our danger. It would not occur to us to question a necessary process, but the discovery of contingency, and thus of our own responsibility for Being's structure, is an unnerving experience which may make us falter as well as prompt us to rise to the occasion. In the encounter with nothingness, and in accounting for the depth of its impact upon us, we may discover our freedom (p. 24). Yet just as nonbeing is a lack or an emptiness, so freedom may isolate us into inactivity. We do not always have to respond to a demand by taking action; we may do nothing. Through questioning, and in investigating the ontological foundation of questioning, we discover the negative element in all Being—the nothingness which is present there—and the response to this is anguish. Fear is fear of beings, but anguish is caused by the recognition of the aspects of nonbeing within Being itself. The result is an anxiousness over our own freedom in this situation, faced as we are with a contingent structure of Being.

What must Being be if human behavior is to have a rational explanation? Questioning, negativity, anguish, decision—all these and more characterize human behavior. A rational explanation of such behavior requires that Being be of such structure that activity like this on the part of human beings is not merely irrational but instead is explained by it, in the sense that such human activity is intelligible as a response to the discovery of Being's structure. I am in anguish precisely because any conduct on my part is only possible, says Sartre (p. 31); and, for such an emotion to be rational, the structure of Being itself must be at least partially characterizable by contingency and nothingness. Then such human behavior would be understandable. Nothing can compel one to act in a certain way, and yet that very fact makes decision difficult, because it is not only something but also nothing which lies behind each human decision. Things, rules, conditions do apply to conduct, but they do not fully determine it, and the element of nothingness in our deliberations is the most difficult part. *Being must contain nothingness for our behavior to be explained. That is how metaphysics is based on experience.*

Freedom separates us from our future (p. 35), because nothingness stands between us and our future self in the sense that we may never become that future self. It is possible for the future to get lost, or at least to be modified, in the nothingness which stands between the present and some planned or desired future. If the future state were necessary, human anguish (i.e., as a response to seeing the self still separated from its future by the possibility of nothingness) would be unintelligible. The prospect of the possible loss of the desired future self, with nothingness replacing it, is one cause of anguish. Yet it is also the source of man's freedom, because it means that nothing, not even his previous state, can compel a man to become his future. The possibility of not becoming one's future self is at once the source of man's freedom "to be or not to be" that future. The possibility of nothingness which induces dread is the very condition for the possibility of becoming one's future freely (p. 37).

"Anguish then is the reflective apprehension of freedom by itself" (p. 39). We have avoided nonbeing, but, upon analysis, it appears again as the very condition for the transcendence of the present state toward our future being. In accounting for the human phenomenon of 'anguish', the presence of nonbeing in Being is uncovered as one metaphysical account which can explain a psychological state. Some metaphysicians (e.g., Spinoza) exclude nonbeing, but then they cannot see anguish and contingency as irreducible phenomenon. If the psychological analysis and the literary account of the existentialists are accepted, we have an empirical ground for insisting that metaphysics must account for nonbeing and its presence within Being. It is true that Spinoza's account of Being without contingency and without any possible lapse is rationally consistent and intelligible. With the existentialist account of psychological states and their literary portrayal of our internal life, however, a new empirical base is provided for a metaphysical analysis of a different quality.

"What must the being of man be if he is to be capable of . . . ?" and "What must Being be if man is to be capable of . . . ?" are the two basic questions for the new mode of metaphysical inquiry opened by the existentialist accounts, whether they fully intended this or not. These questions, as approaches, require metaphysics' use of indirect techniques rather than a direct inquiry into Being's structure. Yet, to balance this difficulty, we have the extensive empirical base provided in the new psychology and literature. Here is a penetrating account of the being of man, and still at the very heart of this account the problem of Being and nonbeing arises. This happens in such a way that the central metaphysical problem is not abstract and detached but is so involved in man's condition that metaphysics actually provides the only basis upon which man can be understood. Metaphysics is not distant from human concerns, but now it is the only basis upon which they may be rationally comprehended. In a metaphysics based on this empirical ground, we do not get certainty and necessity in our theory, but we do get a possible explanation of why man feels and acts as he does. If Being and nonbeing are related as they are here portrayed, man's psychological moods become a rational response to such a basic structure.

If Being and nonbeing can both be accounted for, the nonbeing encountered in the being of man can be explained, although in temporal sequence we first discover the centrality of nonbeing in man according to the existentialist account. Clearly it is both a consideration of the future and the problem of passage from a present stage toward a new future which reveals the presence of nonbeing in man. If we confine ourselves (with the strict empiricist) only to what is present, we do not see this difficult side of man's being; i.e., precisely that side which raises the metaphysical problem of Being and nonbeing. Sartre talks of Being and Nothingness, and Heidegger of Being and Time, but clearly the two concepts are linked. For it is only in the consideration of past and future, and in the precariousness of the passage between them, that the problem of nothingness arises. In the present everything is just what it is; Being is full. When past and future are considered, happiness (which is the ability to live only in the present for a time) passes into anguish as the human self uncovers the problem of nonbeing for metaphysics. Nothingness is discovered in time, and then time uncovers the nothingness which the pure present cannot know.

The past exists for us as nonbeing (p. 109). I am no longer my past and yet I am it. The past is what it is and is closed to possibility, and in that sense it is not as involved in nonbeing as the future is. And yet it is involved in nonbeing in the sense that, fixed and final though it is, it no longer exists as such, as it did when it was present. A form of nonbeing is discovered in considering the relation of the past to our present in that we are separated from our past by a fixed form of nonbeing. But what is more important, we are separated from our future by a form of nonbeing which involves contingency and freedom. That is, we are not free not to be our past, and yet it is separated from us—a fact that sometimes causes anguish. But we are separated from the desired future by the freedom not to be it and by the possibility of losing that future in the nonbeing which lies between the present and the future. Thus, the problem of nonbeing is most acute where the future is concerned. The results of this fact for this beginning of a new metaphysics will be explored further in the Epilogue.

Sartre asserts that, if God exists, he is contingent (p. 81); this is undoubtedly true, although Sartre understandably does not himself pursue this statement. The difficult but crucial distinction between man's contingency and God's we will try to work out in the final chapter (8). The relation to time and the encounter with nonbeing make metaphysicians of both God and man, but man's being is different from God's, and the extent of this difference explains the form of contingency which can be said to be present in God.

A certain venturing into theology in this way becomes necessary if we are to attempt to give an account of the origin of nothingness in Being, the 'why' of its presence. Sartre simply accepts the presence of nonbeing phenomenologically. If, however, we turn from man's being and his encounter with nothingness to Being's structure itself, the question of the origin of nothingness again arises—just as the question of the origin of negation in man arose for Sartre. To pursue this requires an excursion into theology, for we have to examine nonbeing in God's being and then its transmission in the ultimate origination of things. Sartre does not take this step, but there is no reason why someone else may not.

Discovering freedom in the face of nothingness does mean that our metaphysics must be one of contingency and probability *vs.* the classical emphasis on necessity. Yet if the existentialist literature is to serve as the basis for a revived metaphysics, it seems natural that it should have an emphasis that is different from the metaphysics which Kant could not ground empirically. In fact, this leads one to suspect that the reason Kant could not find an empirical base for metaphysics is that the metaphysics which he had in mind was different from a commentary on empirical existence. If we take the existentialist account and build a metaphysics from that, this metaphysics will have features different from Kant's, but (ironically) it will have the empirical base which he demanded. Sartre and his analysis of nothingness force us to abandon certainty. If we abandon certainty as a requirement, we can have a metaphysics of possibility. A demand for necessity seems to mean that metaphysics can never be empirically grounded.

Literature provides a certain form of a priori knowledge, although not quite what Kant had in mind. In reading Sartre's literary works, for example, we learn about experience without actually going through that experience ourselves (see chapter 4). This would not be possible if such literature did not have metaphysical significance, since only if it reveals an abstract structure of Being as present also in us can we understand the reported experience simply by reference to our own internal existence. Internally we grasp via literature the structures in the reported experience which we can discover in ourselves, even though they are not concretely embodied in us. The artist has used his literary skill and power to disclose some structure of human existence which we can then grasp without passing directly through the experience ourselves. Literature of philosophical significance provides a certain form of a priori understanding, although it is without Kant's desired quality of necessity. Were the structures of Being themselves necessary, as

Kant undoubtedly thought, the a priori grasp of them might produce necessity. In the existentialist literature, this does not seem to be the case. Kant was "wrong" about metaphysics because he was "wrong" about Being, not vice versa (i.e., he held a different possible view).

The thesis of chapter 3 was that crises could (*not* must) provide an insight which is unavailable in ordinary experience. A strict empiricist cannot find metaphysics, because his selection of experience is avowedly standard and normal. But how can crisis produce such insight (insight and aberration being, not far apart, but close and both the product of crisis)? Perhaps in Sartre we find an answer. Crises usually involve the encounter with nothingness, in which one can be lost and paralyzed to the point of inaction. But one can also discover in anguish the relation of nonbeing to Being, its presence within Being, and the freedom which this involves. In this respect the crisis can provide insight into the structure of Being itself. And, because in the encounter with the fact of nothingness no specific object is present, the experience is universalizable and applicable to all men. Particular content, which always separates us, is missing, and thus both the crisis and the potential insight can have a universal quality.

Even granting the validity of such subjective insight, how is this turned into an objective insight in Being? That is the traditional question which will still bother many readers. There is no answer possible, if the only answer which will be accepted is one which would demonstrate that Being does have these qualities objectively. The answer which can be given, however, is that Being is not directly accessible, and so techniques of indirection are required (which is a situation common in the physical sciences).

Psychology may be a necessary intermediary here; as a part of Being, we test Being's structure by insight into our own. Using this route one cannot prove that all subjectivity has been eliminated, but one can give an account of Being without subjective reference. Only later do we turn back to see whether such an account explains subjective experience also. The subjective medium is necessary at the outset, but it may be dispensed with. Yet we cannot forget that experience and human structure are not self-explanatory; there must be something which opens them to view too. This the novel and philosophical psychology can do. We must be brought into relation with even our own structure, and this the force of the encounter with nonbeing can accomplish. The profound author's power over words is also explained here: the impact of nothingness and time upon him give him greater power to form his impression; that is, if clarity and not a dazed condition is the result of his encounter.

Ethics and metaphysics are of course brought quite close together in this approach. It is not so simple as to say that metaphysics has an ethical base; what is true is that, in all ethical situations of crucial import, metaphysical structure can be revealed—and must be—if the element of freedom is to be understood and the situation faced. In nothingness and in time, metaphysics and ethics are brought together. For, without an understanding of nothingness and its presence within Being, the basis for freedom and contingency cannot be grasped and the situation met with full knowledge. Spinoza offers us the classical example of an ethics with a metaphysical base, but he begins with God and not from human psychology, as the existentialists have. Constructing a metaphysics from their material, we get an account of freedom and contingency which is different from Spinoza's metaphysics, and perhaps it also results in a more relevant contemporary ethics.

Has Sartre perhaps provided us with a possible answer to the three questions we posed on page 45, and which were taken to be central to the thesis of this small volume? There we asked: How is literature in the philosophical sense—that is, concerning metaphysical insight—possible? If the existentialists have provided the prolegomena to metaphysics which Kant demanded (although admittedly and ironically, to a different metaphysics), it will be due to the fact that the literature which they have produced is agreed to contain philosophical relevance and because their psychological explorations are accepted as leading to a metaphysical grasp. In our explorations of Sartre, this is what we have attempted to show, although "The Origin of Negation" has been our main interest here, not his dramatic works directly. In the experiences of man, can the presence of nonbeing be brought to the surface in literature in a way in which ordinary sense experience would pass over it? If so, the recognition of the presence of nonbeing is mediated via literature and can lead on to the classical metaphysical quest to determine the relation of nonbeing to Being.

The question abstractly posed on page 44 should be considered concretely in the context of the existentialist literature from Kierkegaard to Camus. Anxiety and dread are portrayed there, and, if this literary treatment brings them to a full recognition and leads to an exploration of Being's structure in an attempt to explain their pervasive presence, literature will have been established as possible in a philosophical mode. The techniques of the writer must produce a literary insight into structures which are basic even to those whose circumstances are different from the author's characters. Self-reflection is induced. The energy transferred from the author's words (formed in his impact with nonbeing) is turned into insight, and Being's structure is thus reflected indirectly. The *via negativa* requires that we be able to experience more than what our own direct senses can afford us, and here a philosophical literature is our primary source.

Heidegger and Time

How is it that in our day 'time' has emerged as a major metaphysical problem? Any reply to this question should begin by pointing out that 'time' has always been a central metaphysical problem. We can rephrase our question, then: At the end of an era in which direct metaphysical construction has been challenged and sometimes halted, how has the concentration upon 'time' made possible new metaphysical construction which meets the demand for an empirical ground? The nothingness which Sartre encountered was primarily in the not-being of the past and the future. Now Heidegger proposes that Being be approached via time. Both use the existentialist literature as a base and both use heavily psychological terms as a medium for metaphysical construction. Both also change the conception of the task of metaphysics. In some sense 'freedom' has really become the central question for contemporary metaphysics, but our concern here is that the explanation of nothingness and time has now been based upon immediate experience. Through this process freedom has emerged as a central issue; at least it is our contemporary approach to Being without necessity and certainty.

Asking questions is the mode of being which Heidegger also gives to man through which Being is to be understood. Because it begins with man's being, Heidegger can call the question of being "the most basic and the most concrete" (p. 29).[2] We are now in the midst of things, and through our being, Being is disclosed, since the understanding of Being is a characteristic of our own being. But we understand our own being in terms of possibility (p. 33). Does this mean that Being can only be understood in terms of possibility? No, but it does mean that possibility will be *our* means of approach to an understanding of Being. We possess in our own being an understanding of the Being of all entities (p. 58), partly because we are the being which has its own being at issue. Our own being does not just simply exist; it must consider possibilities, and this involves us in the necessity of understanding Being through possibility and probability.

'Concern' characterizes our kind of being (p. 83), and again the possibility of a psychology with philosophic import is a necessary first question if the use of such terms is to open the way to a new metaphysics. Our being reveals itself as 'care' (p. 227), and the phenomenon of anxiety is basic to such a metaphysical analysis. Heidegger is convinced that we do not in our day understand the meaning of 'being' and that 'time' should form the basis for our exploration. Time functions as a criterion for distinguishing realms of Being (p. 39). Of course, many philosophers have said this, from Plato on, and only Heidegger's existential context can be considered novel in our era. What

2 All page references in this section (except as indicated) are to Heidegger, *Being and Time*, ed. John McIntyre and Ian Ramsey; trans. John MacQuarrie and Edward Robinson (London: SCM Press, 1962).

Hume missed when he did not see the connection of every aspect of being is the pervasive structure of time which holds the past and future together with the present.

The past is in some sense still present (p. 430), but only in the mode of not being. Time can never be exhausted by the present, although Heidegger admits that time's primary characteristic is the "now." Time involves both past and future; both exist, although never as present. Nonbeing will become primary on such an analysis, and the unique feature which distinguishes this basis for metaphysics is that it approaches Being via nonbeing, nothingness, and negativity.

Perhaps the most sophisticated classical account of nonbeing is Plato's *Sophist*, but Plato makes nonbeing there into a mode of Being, primarily 'otherness'. In a classical analysis nonbeing is never taken as primary, and the psychological exploration of human states seldom forms the data for metaphysics. The revolution in the contemporary existentialist prolegomena to a contemporary metaphysics is the empirical grounding which nonbeing is given in psychological analysis and in literary exploration. This approach misses the necessity and certainty which abstract speculation always seemed to seek. Pure reason sought a different form of metaphysical certainty and could never ground it. The existential grounding enables us to give an account of Being, but only through the analysis of nonbeing, that is, when it is taken as primary.

In response to Kant, Heidegger stressed the finite nature of man and attempted to indicate how transcendence could be possible.[3] The specific finitude of human nature is decisive to the problem of metaphysics. Were man not finite, metaphysics would not be necessary (see discussion in chapter 8). Were man not finite, metaphysics would also be impossible, since it springs from the conditions of finitude. The problem here is the specific finitude of the human subject (p. 177, *K&PM*). Time as such is the character of selfhood. Because of the nature of human finitude, time is primordial to it. And, because human finitude

---

3 See my article, "Heidegger and the Problem of Metaphysics," *Philosophy and Phenomenological Research*, 24, no. 3 (March, 1964): 410–16, based on Heidegger's *Kant and the Problem of Metaphysics (K&PM)*, trans. James S. Churchill (Bloomington, Ind.: Indiana University Press, 1962). The page references which follow are to this volume and are designated *K&PM*.

necessitates metaphysics, an analysis of the primordial nature of time is central to metaphysics and in fact provides its foundation. What is crucial here, Heidegger feels, is that time always has an orientation toward the future.

Time forms the essential structure of subjectivity (p. 194, *K&PM*), and to be a subject means to possess the power of being solicited by objects other than the self. To be a self means to be dependent on receptivity and to possess in itself a temporal character. Time and thought are the same. The ego is time itself and, unless time is its very essence, it cannot be at all (p.198, *K&PM*). Time in turn forms the basis for the imagination, since to possess creative imagination means to express the future, and time is itself future-oriented. We are able to transcend the present precisely because the imagination is rooted in time. Because of our ability to transcend the present through the function of imagination, ontological knowledge is made possible. "Primordial time lets the sure formation of transcendence take place" (p. 202, *K&PM*).

Heidegger's analysis of Kant led him to the transcendental imagination. The root of this capacity he finds in primordial time. The foundation of metaphysics is revealed by Kant to be time (p. 207, *K&PM*). Since the foundation of metaphysics is discovered to be vested in a quality of man, however, developing metaphysics will mean an interrogation of man, and this demands that metaphysics begin with an anthropology. ". . . only a philosophic anthropology can undertake the laying of the foundation of true philosophy . . ." (P. 215, *K&PM*.) Philosophical anthropology inquires into the essence of man and in that sense becomes a "regional ontology" (p. 218, *K&PM*). Human subjectivity turns out to be at the very center of the metaphysical problems.

Because man is what he is, metaphysics is both demanded and made possible, and because his essence remains mysterious the problem is preserved, continued, and reworked anew from old foundations. Yet the disclosure of the temporality of man's essence, plus the transcendence and future orientation it implies, renders metaphysics possible. An omnipotent being need not question himself, his nature, and his capacities, but man's finite nature requires this questioning, and thus it establishes metaphysics. By questioning itself, human nature reveals its finitude and its concern with its finitude (p. 224, *K&PM*). Human reason is this very concern about its ability to be finite. The finitude of man itself becomes a problem, and this is both metaphysics' foundation and its first problem.

How to approach this question is the first issue of metaphysics, and this in itself involves metaphysics, since basically the question of human finitude is answered by bringing to light the essential connection between Being as such and the finitude of man. Metaphysics is both demanded and given its ground in the fact that man can understand the limitations of his nature only by placing himself within the general structure of Being, and it is the delineation of these structures which traditionally has been metaphysics. "What is the essence of man as a knowing subject?" forces us back to the question of being as such and then beyond that to ask how we are to comprehend a structure such as that of Being. Discovering in philosophical anthropology man's essential temporality allows man to transcend himself and to discover Being as time—or so Heidegger's argument runs.

By studying man, we discover that he already possesses in his nature an understanding of Being. He still lacks the concepts, and to suggest possible concepts to express his natural grasp is the function of metaphysics. Man's existence means this comprehension of Being, which means that metaphysics is rooted in and develops from the existence of man (p. 225, *K&PM*). The ground of human existence provides man with his comprehension of Being. Metaphysics is every question relating to a human finitude to whose constitution the comprehension of Being belongs. Discovering a foundation for metaphysics turns out to be a metaphysics itself (p. 238, *K&PM*), since it is not possible to discover the foundation without discovering man and his relation to Being as such.

The primordial metaphysical fact is that the essence of human finitude is constantly known without being understood. We are aware of our condition but we forget it, so that metaphysics becomes a remembering and a wresting from forgetfulness that essential knowledge of Being which it primordially comprehends. We know our condition in a latent manner even when we are forgetful, so that recovery and explication are basic metaphysical tools (p. 242, *K&PM*). Existential analysis discloses a transcendence of the subject, since a subject cannot be without grasping what it means to be in the world. From this our knowledge of Being can be understood only as relative to time, and this gives 'time' primary status as a metaphysical problem.

We begin and end with the problem of human finitude. Nothing is so radically opposed to ontology as the idea of an infinite being (p. 254, *K&PM*), so that man generates metaphysics only because he is not God. God may be redefined as the being who understands himself without the aid of such theoretical structures. Only a being whose existence is limited, and threatened because it is limited by being placed in the midst of others, develops a metaphysics. To be limited means primarily to be essentially temporal; but, since time has a future orientation, through it man in knowing himself as temporal actually escapes the present. His existence in the midst of other beings involves an implicit grasp of what being itself must be, if only he can recover this knowledge and make it explicit in metaphysical theory. Man's finitude poses the problem; and, properly understood, a knowledge of his essence may solve it; i.e., may give metaphysics its ground.

We now ask one concluding question: If finitude involved not only limitation (being surrounded by time and its transcendence) but also freedom, would even God (although not subject to the problems of finitude) require metaphysics as a theoretical basis to comprehend both his own and finite freedom? (For a more complete discussion of this issue see chapter 8.) This might prove that metaphysics, although associated intimately with time and limitation, arises in God (and also in man) chiefly from his freedom and his unconscious understanding of its operation. Man's freedom in action and in thought forces him to transcend himself and to attempt to understand both his own finite nature and the structure of Being within which he operates.

Both God and man may do this by creating a theoretical structure outside themselves, and sometimes this leads them to become metaphysicians. God is always a metaphysician eternally embracing all possible theoretical structures but producing only one. Man is both forced by his nature and given the ground from his finite nature to transcend himself and to produce metaphysical structures, but his theories lack the singularity of God's, because he lacks God's power of decision. Thus the human theoretical task was and is and ever continues to be. Essential freedom in the Divine nature makes theory possible; human finitude makes theory at the same time possible, necessary, and never certain or complete.

Neither Heidegger nor Sartre has explicitly attempted a revival of classical metaphysics as such, although this may be what they have in fact prepared the way for. Both have come very close to traditional theological issues, and yet they have never spoken very directly about God. If such existential analysis has really opened a new ground for theology,[4] we should be able to take this material and draw some conclusions about the being of God. Time and nonbeing are the interpretative concepts. In what sense are these applicable to God and what can we learn by applying them? To attempt a brief answer here is important to the construction of a new metaphysics if we are to provide it on an existentialist base.

In another work[5] Heidegger is aware that time produces itself only insofar as man is, so that there is no time where man is not. This being the case, God cannot be approached temporally without assuming that he shares man's structure, which cannot be disclosed from an examination of man alone. Thus, it is particularly true, where God is concerned, that the approach via time faces a challenge, just as all metaphysical categories meet their severest test when God is described. Perhaps, as Hans Jonas suggests,[6] "The understanding of God is not to be reduced to the self-understanding of man."

If, as Heidegger himself begins to develop the idea elsewhere,[7] being is questioned only as a means to induce the encounter with the complete other of Being (the nothingness belonging to Being), perhaps we investigate the subjective structure of man only to discover his nonbeing (although his being is temporal in

4 For a more extended discussion, see my article "Heidegger, Time and God," *Journal of Religion*, 47, no. 4 (October, 1967): 279–94.

5 *An Introduction to Metaphysics*, trans. Ralph Manheim (Garden City, N.Y.: Anchor Books, 1961).

6 "Heidegger and Theology," *Review of Metaphysics*, 18, no. 2 (December, 1964): 232.

7 *The Question of Being*, trans. William Kluback and Jean T. Wilde (New York: Twayne Publishers, 1958).

structure). It might also be that man's nonbeing appears most evident in his relation to God, because time is eliminated and the nothingness which is discovered in the divine nature will expose God's nontemporality and also man's. "Nonbeing and time" is a volume which can not be written except as a contrast, since nonbeing discloses an absence of time.

If the experience of nonbeing (e.g., dread rather than concern) is taken as the interpretive center for the being of man, perhaps time is not Being's center and human nature could more easily be related to the Divine, since the deepest religious experience is that of being 'nothing' before God. Morally this is felt as unworthiness, and it is, in Kierkegaard's favorite phrase, to feel yourself against God as being "always in the wrong." How many possible modes of Being are there, and to how many is man's positive nature the key? If the core of Being is hidden and requires "disclosure" (to reborrow Heidegger's borrowed theological term), then perhaps its center is not in the obvious place—i.e., in its Being (its temporality)—but in its nonbeing, the experience of which is illuminating but is not to be described in temporal terms. Heidegger's famous radical question (Why is there any Being at all—why not far rather nothing? [8]) actually comes much closer than time to disclosing Being, so that *not time but its absence and the experience of nonbeing* could be the major key to our needed contemporary metaphysics.

Finite beings are dependent on intuition, which is essentially temporal.[9] But is our nature exclusively finite, or is the experience of nonbeing essentially a disclosure of our nonlimited core (the realization of which would certainly be enough to frighten a being with only a limited power of control)? The impact of nonbeing is a nontemporal experience that removes us from sense intuition and opens Being to a nontemporal understanding. Time is limited to the data of internal sense, but are we so restricted in every aspect of our being? Or do we transcend our finite selves under the threat of nonbeing, so that we understand ourselves and Being in a moment of existential crisis in a way that the temporal sequence of life can never reveal?

8 *Existence and Being* (Chicago: Henry Regnery Co., 1949) , p. 380.
9 *Kant and the Problem of Metaphysics*, p. 39.

Is temporal thinking really as fundamental to man as it casually appears, or is time fundamental only if we begin with an analysis of sense experience? Thought in its speculative aspect has a time of its own, if indeed it is not out of all time. Yet such a speculative standpoint beyond time may in fact be the best vantage point from which to understand both being and time, so that the shock produced in an experience of the threat of nonbeing has its counterpart in the exhilaration of speculative thought that knows no restriction to time. Then the self might not be temporal in its inmost essence,[10] although it could appear so until the shell of the self is penetrated by an encounter with nonbeing. When the self is threatened, its core is disclosed and time will have a stop.

When Heidegger does turn to consider God directly, he finds the notion of "cause of itself" most meaningful,[11] but he rightly sees this God as bringing thought to a halt. Such a God cannot be approached with a temporal framework only. When man is not the object of the metaphysician's exclusive preoccupation, this would seem to say that when God is considered directly some of our anthropological prejudices must fall. Verbal thought must always move (and so must physical men), but, when we encounter such a notion of God, silence seems—at least at first—to be a more appropriate mode of thought.

This "thinkingless God" might perhaps be a better clue to Being's center than the restless and constantly moving thought of man. Can we begin metaphysics at this point? Or, more appropriately, what mode of man's being can, if disclosed, lead us to such an understanding of God? Perhaps the psychic shock of an encounter with nonbeing might do this, but certainly not the temporal regularity of sense experience. What part of man's being is able to lead to a disclosure of God's nature, and how might this explain the temporal and its relation to God and man? In our day we need to discover the conditions for God's disclosure.

Since Heidegger approached Being via time, it naturally comes to mind to ask whether a different avenue is open to us. If we are

10 *Ibid.*, p. 200.
11 *Essays in Metaphysics*, trans. Kurt F. Leidecker (New York: Philosophical Library, 1961), pp. 65–66.

to find this, we must conduct an existential psychological exploration of some aspect of experience that impresses us as being atemporal, i.e., outside the temporal structure. A crisis situation occurring when existence is threatened by an encounter with nonbeing which produces anxiety and dread seems to have a nontemporal aspect. When we are set apart from Being and the ongoing temporality of life rather than being just part of its continuous process, perhaps nontemporality can be understood.

Abnormal experiences can provide our release from time; average, normal experiences are always embraced by time. The unexpected can release us and may prove to have a metaphysical and theological significance out of all proportion to its numerical weight among our experiences, although its psychological impact is such that its weight in this respect is enormous. In the experiences which interrupt life and bring it to a sudden halt, we may also experience nontemporality (no past, no future, only present) and thus have open to us an approach to Being without time.

We have now come to question whether the self is always temporal in its self-understanding. It probably is, in its dealings with sense data and inanimate objects. With itself, and in certain revelatory personal encounters, the self enters a realm in which time is missing, although in its approach it may still be aware of time. Yet in addition to these crucial psychological experiences and as a counterpart to them, the mind in its speculative employment can operate out of relation to time. Mathematical entities (the consideration of possible modes of being) are in themselves theoretical operations which do not accommodate to time; that is, until the possible concrete embodiment of such speculative thought comes under consideration.

In fact, it seems that some creative minds are employed more here than in the temporal order, and all minds have at least a partial occupation out of time and understand the importance of this exception to the temporal structure for the entities which they consider. There are, then, objects and ways of knowing directed to them which are not essentially temporal. Kant did not trust these modes, but they have become increasingly important as the sciences have turned heavily theoretical, and mathematics seems only partially concerned with the empirical world.

Perhaps Plato is right—that knowledge is not accomplished until we escape from time. Perhaps it is also true that although the mind concerns itself with temporal process, the mind still is not at its core temporal, although it can and most often does reflect this mode. We have an existential psychology now supporting a Platonic ontology. Perhaps phenomena are not primary but secondary. If so, the mind would actually have an initial orientation toward nontemporal entities (the possible modes of Being) and would consider the particular embodiment of these only secondarily, the point at which time enters experience. Do we ever consider nontemporal entities without relating them to temporal phenomena? The existentialists have given us psychological reasons for answering yes, in which case it might be that time is secondary even in thought. This neither Kant nor the Platonists considered, although each for quite different reasons. If Being is understood only in the contrast provided by nonbeing as it is encountered in an unusual experience that always comes as a shock and breaks the bond of time, then nonbeing can be primary, and it may yield a nontemporal approach to God.

Yet what if the mind itself is primarily temporally oriented? Would it still be impossible for us to understand structures whose ontological mode is basically different from our own? Much of the time we assume that like can only know like, that if our mind is temporal so also must its objects be. Yet perhaps this is not always true. Perhaps the mind lives by adapting to modes of being other than its own, in which case even its own temporal bias (if true) would not preclude its grasp in knowledge of nontemporal modes. In fact, it could be that genuine knowledge takes place only when there is a shock produced by the contrast between the temporal and the nontemporal modes of being.

Were all modes similarly constituted ontologically, perhaps only the gathering of data would be possible and not the insight of knowledge. The mind may record, but it does not reach and grasp, except when it is shocked from its basis by a violence of contrasts. The mind lives among modes of being, but it comes to understand Being only in the contrasting experience with nonbeing. The mind moves in time, but perhaps it achieves the insight of knowledge only when it encounters nontemporal modes of being. Nontemporal entities alone can make time real and awaken the understanding. If this is true, it might make possible a new understanding of God.

The stress upon time and the dominance of its structures derives from the subjective orientation which has preoccupied philosophy for several generations. Yet Kierkegaard, who is notorious for his stress upon the subjective approach, is aware that there is no subjective problem unless there is first of all an objective issue. In parallel fashion, perhaps we cannot be aware of time except in contrast to an awareness of nontemporal entities. Time, then, cannot be internally understood or even brought to awareness except through the experience of the non-temporal.

The outlines of our context do not become clear until a shock breaks us through the barrier and we are aware of time's absence or end, which explains the existentialists' stress on the philosophical efficacy of death. When such a shattering encounter with nonbeing breaks in and takes us out of time, we become painfully aware of time; but it is just as true that reflections upon such experiences might reveal our grasp of, and relationship to, nontemporal modes of being. When time is "broken," it is finally understood. Nonbeing is not "against God," but it opens Being and God to an understanding that is not exclusively temporal.

Can God know directly a sequence in time without being temporal in his own nature? This is perhaps the most crucial question for theology. And we are now in a position to give an answer: if time is not an all-embracing form which envelops all types of experience and all modes of being but is instead merely a by-product of change, then (if like may know unlike, as we have argued) God may be directly aware of change and yet not necessarily be involved in change himself. For this to be possible, God's nature must be of a certain type, but this is not the place to set that out in detail.[12]

12 For a further development of this issue, see my *Divine Perfection: Possible Ideas of God* (New York: Harper & Bros., 1953).

God must encompass within himself all possible modes and also be aware of their every possible combination, so that, when certain states are in fact actualized, he will then come to know the actual existence of what he always knew as possible. In this respect his knowledge changes, but this is not so extensive as to involve his nature itself in change too. God remains unchanged in his nature and nothing new comes under his vision, except the knowledge that certain possibles are actualized for a time, in certain patterns and combinations.

Just as man needs the sharp contrast of the nontemporal in order to become fully aware of time, so God understands eternally because he also understands how man understands in part in time. God understands himself as opposed to time by knowing it as his creation and by understanding himself as defined against it. Not at every temporal alteration, but in the act of creation, God alters himself; although the limitation involved in a specific creation is a voluntary one and an act which God freely takes upon himself. God observes change directly but is not himself directly changed. No new concept is added, only the awareness of something eternally understood as now actually existing. Although he did not know of this existence with certainty, he knew it as possible from eternity before man actualized it.

Change is more basic than time, and God apprehends factual change in his knowledge without being changed himself, so that he knows time in the objects of the world but not as within his own nature (except in the act of creation and cessation). God may know time without being it. God has within himself the power which everything has to become, but this is not temporal, although the being which does become is. God knows the rules which govern the actualization of any combination of possibles, but not that they must exist in such a way. This factor time adds, but it is not a radically new knowledge. Actualization for God cannot be the upsetting encounter with the unknown that it often is for a man.

Is time not really central but simply a derivative of change ("passing away and coming to be"), so that in a being powerful enough to prevent this in his own nature (God) no time would be present except in the knowledge of time as applicable to others? Time enters as a by-product into a nature without the power and the will to hold the elements of its nature under decisive control and at rest, as God can do. Movement indicates loss of control, and time is the manifestation of this, although it is not necessarily characteristic of Being-itself.

God moved once in creation when his will concluded, and he can move again to halt the process (although Christians assert one additional intermediate movement). Just as this decisive but once-and-for-all movement relates him to time, so his knowledge of it is received without the necessity of further alteration. Our acquired knowledge changes us, because it often concerns modes of being which were not previously apprehended (which is never true of God), and because we are not powerful enough or fixed enough in will not to allow our nature to be altered by new knowledge. God is able to absorb without essential change. What is presented to him as actual he eternally knows as possible. Such additional information would induce change in us and produce time; God can accept without response, although he can also respond if he wills to do so.

If God does receive the knowledge of change impassively, we might be led to suspect one further essential feature of his nature: his mode of communication can be silence. If silence and not conversation or dialogue (of course, in our dialogue a man may speak God's part for him) is God's central characteristic, he neither speaks in dialectically complicated sentences nor requires time as central to his nature or even as indigenous to our knowing relation to him. When God is most truly known, change, time, and all conversation cease, an experience many mystics have reported. Such silence on God's part is also what has led some to experience "the death of God."

Change and time appear to move around him but not to touch him, and his silent core leaves man the maximum freedom for his own self-directed change. Silence is his answer to questions, and oddly enough a great many answers can be deduced from this important fact. His silence in response to our interrogation can indicate just how different God's nature is from ours, so that we may now attempt to construct what these differences would have to be: to know time and yet not to be in time; to understand changes not of his specific origination and yet not to be changed by this. We can now sketch out in what ways God would have to differ from man in order for this to be true.

Plato came to see the importance of specifying nonbeing's relation to Being, and he found the two to be close, not far apart. Nonbeing, when explored by the existentialists, has shocked us out of time and made the understanding of a God who is different from man possible for us once again. Yet for this to be possible, nonbeing must have a crucial status in the divine nature itself. Psychologically we experience nonbeing as real, but that is because man can change and pass out of existence. What about God and nonbeing? Since God's being involves all the possible modes of Being, of which only a small portion are actualized, any experience of the divine nature must feel and be impressed by the nonbeing of all the nonactualized possibles. Time does not itself apply to God except in his knowledge, since no change is present, and thus man experiences God's nature as nonbeing in relation to his own human mode of being.

Power and perfect will combine to such overwhelming proportions and stand in such violent contrast to God's silence that man will seem to be swallowed up in nonbeing whenever he discovers his own being's relation to God. To nonbeing, time cannot apply (except in its change into some specific form of being) ; so that, to the vast and silent wastelands of God's nature, time is unreal and is not applicable. And in discovering this, man can come to realize the rather limited applicability of time—a fact which he can discover from his own nature only when it is in a state of crisis. Psychological crisis is induced by the inbreaking of the vastness of the divine nonbeing, which is an experience that human power is hardly equal to. To come up against this is to be changed in our mode of being and knowing.

The Sense of 'Proof' [13]

In what sense can it be said that the thesis offered here has been "proven"? That of course depends on what one means by 'proof'.

13 For a parallel discussion, see my "The Meaning of 'Proof' in Anselm's Ontological 'Argument'," *Journal of Philosophy*, 64, no. 15 (August 10, 1967) : 459–86.

Certainly we have not established metaphysics on this basis alone, with only these problems admitted and with only one theoretical structure possible that excludes all others. If the structure of Being is like what we have inferred, and if metaphysics is the kind of enterprise which we have described— then this, in the nature of the case, would be impossible. The flexibility and freedom within Being is itself the basis upon which alternative theoretical structures which describe it remain possible too. Our language structure is not identical with Being's structure; this too adds flexibility to the variety of metaphysical views which are possible. This being so, we can never mean by 'proof' in metaphysics that some single doctrine has been established as true with necessity and certainty. That security is now forbidden to us after centuries of seeking. Since Being is not characterized by these attributes either, theory about it cannot be certain. Certainty and necessity are possible within a given framework provided the axioms of that framework are accepted. But in metaphysics it is our business to explore all the alternative first principles for various theoretical contexts, so that we can never remain comfortably within one assumed context holding on to our 'proof'.

Is every assertion possible within a metaphysics such as we have proposed here, or has this argument still established some standard to judge importance? It has indicated that perhaps one reason why metaphysics has not often been constructed since Kant's *Prolegomena* is that we have demanded certainty where it is not possible. And the psychological and literary material of the existentialists has been offered as a key toward an insight into Being which is made available in this form when it is not available in another mode. The 'proof' of this new existentialist prolegomena which makes the elaboration of the metaphysics possible is that within its terms a description of Being in general can be constructed. It can be shown to be a consistent doctrine and to offer an explanation of the world's structure as we find it. It can be extended from psychology and literature to a systematic use. The 'proof' is that it is possible to construct a metaphysics and that it can be found to correspond with what we know. Moreover, it can have ethical and clinical applications and extensions.

Two questions are central in this 'proof': "How can we extend ourselves from psychological being to Being itself and be sure that this move is legitimate?" and "Can we accept medical and ethical usefulness as a form of proof?" As to the first, clearly we begin with an internal state, and the literary material of novels and plays, we have argued, really is needed to make our internal life visible. There is, of course, no reason why what we find psychologically insightful should not extend to Being, but this depends on the conviction that Being has the same general structure which our internal life also has.

We have, we think, given some indication that the same qualities can be attributed to both forms of being, although this requires a basic 'univocity' in Being. Being itself cannot have radically different modes from the psychological being which we have described existentially. Demanding different characteristics for Being itself leads to excluding psychological data as a base and to demanding a necessity which is not present in experience. If the existentialist material is to serve as a metaphysical prolegomenon, it will restrict the kind of metaphysics which can be constructed. Even accepting this, how can one tell when he has just another theory and when that particular metaphysical view might really be true or at least close to the truth?

The answer to this involves our second question. The growth of the movement of existential psychoanalysis and the adaptation of existentialist terms for religious purposes both give us a practical confirmation that the theoretical views which are built on this base do seem to have a practical application. We ask: Does the possible metaphysics, which is built upon existentialist literature and psychology, have ethical import? Spinoza began with God and ended with recommendations for conduct. Not being able to be certain of only one view of God, we begin with the immediacy of psychological insight and with a literary analysis of human nature. Then we draw insight from these characteristics with which to define Being itself. Next, in order to check a view that is so constructed, we draw out the ethical implications of such a metaphysics and attempt to determine how practical such advised conduct seems to be in our world. We 'prove' by reattaching the abstract metaphysics to the concrete life. Medically, ethically, and religiously we seem to have ground upon which to extend the existentialist metaphysics.

Of course, just as Kant insisted that this is only a prolegomenon and not the full metaphysics itself, so full 'proof' waits upon the attempt to construct upon this base a solution to all the traditional ethical, religious, and theological problems. The existentialists themselves have shied from doing this, Kierkegaard vociferously, while Sartre and Tillich and Heidegger each moved toward it cautiously and seldom very directly. But what we have wanted to produce here is not the completed metaphysics which could be tested fully, but simply a conclusion which is different from Kant's *Prolegomena;* namely, that we are now in a position in which it seems fruitful to attempt to construct directly a contemporary metaphysics. As we have argued, its 'proof' can be tested only after the construction, and then in its application. The evidence does seem substantial that we are now in possession of a sufficiently large and fruitful body of empirical data, produced without that direct intention by the existentialist, to proceed directly to metaphysical construction without delay, doing our testing afterwards and not before. The resulting metaphysics will be different, we can already tell, from what Kant envisaged, but perhaps the negative conclusions of Kant's own prolegomena are partly due to his demanding a metaphysics which cannot exist in fact. If so, this tells us something both about Being and metaphysics.

What we have 'proved' is that it is now possible to ask certain questions by formulating them in ways which were not envisaged before. 'Nothingness' might not seem to be a fruitful ground; and yet the encounter with it, induced by existentialist psychology, does provide the shock that can produce a transcendence of our ordinary structures. The negative approach to Being via nonbeing proves to be the form which our metaphysical questions take today. 'Time' is an ancient issue, and yet its foundation in terms which are tinged with emotion (e.g., 'care') can lead us to give a rational account of that side of human life which we normally consider nonrational, so that by this an unexpected avenue of insight is opened to time's structure.

Our 'proof' takes the form of new data in immediate

experience which produces a change in our approach and thus in the metaphysical questions which we are led to ask in our own era. We are in the day of Freud and Jung, each of whom began with what apparently was irrational and built a rational account on the basis of this abnormal behavior. Our new metaphysics, too, begins with non-being rather than Being. By doing so, it builds a new account of Being on the basis of previously rejected empirical data. What once was rejected as irrational can on the existentialists' account become a new basis for rational understanding.

7

Tractatus
Metaphysico-Theologicus

A Metaphysical Outline

We have maintained that this is not a full metaphysical account but merely the new prolegomena to its possibility. Yet one way to demonstrate musical accomplishment, short of a full concert, is to play a brief melody. One way to prove that a new metaphysics is possible is to outline some of it.[1] What follows in this chapter, then, is a brief excursion into a capsule metaphysical view.

Our chapter title is, the reader will recognize, a "revision" of Wittgenstein's short work. In the British empirical tradition, which earlier in this century burst forth into logical positivism, it was Wittgenstein who turned the interest back toward metaphysics, but only to metaphysics of a certain kind. Perhaps not all his followers will agree, or recognize his interest as being in line with classical metaphysical construction, but the *Tractatus* is itself in many ways a brief metaphysics. One way to prove this is to follow his form but to vary the assertions offered, thus indicating that the form of the work is compatible with views which differ from Wittgenstein's and that it must therefore be defended against its alternatives; i.e., as one among a series of views compatible with that basis.

What does this tell us? That the views of the *Tractatus* stand

1 Cf. the more detailed discussion of this matter in chapter 5.

merely as one set of assertions amid the possibility of quite different doctrines. Thus Wittgenstein's view, as well as any other alternative, needs to be grounded in some considerations which might indicate whether the actual world is more like Wittgenstein's description or closer to some other alternative abstract sketch. The alteration of Kant's philosophical structure produced this *Existentialist Prolegomena,* so that an opposition to Wittgenstein's thought just might yield an avenue to the new constructive metaphysics itself. That such a route (i.e., revising another man's structure) is required does indicate something about the difficulty and the indirection which are necessary in any approach to Being. We must always stand upon another man's effort in order to ground our own. But if a new metaphysics is now actually possible, this should be able to be done, so what follows here is a short "metaphysical demonstration."

Preface to the Task [2]

Although it is true that what can be said can be said clearly, the logic of our language is such that we cannot know that this permits us to say everything that we need to. The symbolic quality of language, however, does enable us to refer to (to direct attention toward) that which is beyond language, perhaps even to what is beyond its ultimate grasp. The result is that, while what is said within a language can be said perfectly clearly, language may also refer beyond itself to structures which either are not clear in themselves or else are not so clear to us.

In this instance, it is possible for the logical structure of the language to remain clear while its impact on the hearer remains clouded by that to which the language directs him beyond itself. In this sense, what can be said cannot always be said clearly. Yet when we use language clearly—i.e., to refer to something beyond itself which is not equally clear—we must always explain fully

2 Cf. my article, "Tractatus Metaphysico-Theologicus," *Modern Schoolman,* 41, no. 4 (May, 1964): 366–75.

the reasons for our enforced partial silence. Religious language is born from grasping the reasons for such silence; metaphysical discourse comes from the determination to speak clearly anyway.

Thus, we learn that the limits set upon thought are not as narrow as the limits set upon language; and the limits which are set upon the verbal expression of thought fall somewhere in between, since language is able to refer to even that which it cannot adequately express. The result here is to observe that we can set a limit to language because we can think on both sides of such a limit, while on the other hand we cannot similarly set a limit for thought since this could only be done by coming up against what cannot be thought. In this area, between the logical limits of language and the ultimate failure of thought, all metaphysics and theological speculation (as well as most religious experience) lies. In the proper sense of the word, they are both meta-languages; that is, they "think beyond" the basic language structure and report back into it clearly what thought learns through testing its own limits. Language ought to stop with clarity; thought ends where it is finally forced into silence.

The truth of any expression, then, may be determined in relation to its possibility, and it can then be assigned a degree of probability. But, since thought varies in the extent to which it can go beyond language before being reduced to silence, it is often possible to determine the truth of any proposition *within* the language; although the truth of any theory *about* the language itself and its limits cannot be so firmly fixed. As to the truth of the theory here communicated, it seems to me to be a likely one. Possibly it can even be definitive for a time. The analyst who moves within the language structure may reach an essentially final solution, but any metaphysician or theologian must rest content with providing only a possible solution. Their language is such that they cannot express anything more definitive than this.

The value of this brief chapter, then, should consist in the fact that we can, by explicating one possible view, show at the same time how many other possible solutions remain unexplored. It could be otherwise only if we could know whether or not language is able to express everything that is, as well as all that is not. Unfortunately we can never reach this conclusion by the internal study of any language and its particular forms of expression.

A View of the World

The world can be said to be everything that has become the case. We understood this by comprehending what might have been the case had the elements been different or differently organized, how the present situation developed, and what this allows as both possible and probable for the future. An organic whole has been, and is being, formed out of the totality of all possible states. At any given moment our world has become a totality of facts for that time, and these can be ascertained by factual tests; but this totality could never be also the totality of all possible entities. Language works upon facts, whereas thought is oriented more toward possible entities. What can in fact form our world is determined by what is compossible, and this involves all the facts which could be possible for our world, as well as all that are possible for us, but by no means all that are per se possible. The task of metaphysical language is to express the various forms of possibility.

This totality of all that is possible will determine, through its internal laws, what may become a fact and also what cannot become a fact in our given world. This totality of possibles exists in logical space and contains within itself all possible factual worlds. Within our own world, we may divide it also into fact and possible. Any possible within this framework can either become a fact or not become a fact depending upon the operation of causal powers. Every other possible entity would still remain just what it is, although our factual structure would be altered in one direction or another. The real world is this relationship between fact and possible. To express the origin and the ultimate goal of this relationship is the continuing task of religious discourse.

Possible and Actual Entities

What is possible and what can become an actual fact in our world's structure both come out of the existence of an absolutely infinite set of possibles which are continuously present in logical space. This absolutely infinite set of possibles is the combination of every entity or object which could conceivably come into factual existence without an internal contradiction. It is essential that any entity or object which comes into factual existence be at the same time a constituent part of this absolutely infinite set of possibles. Every fact has, in this sense, a dual life, a dual existence, a double set of relations. Language is therefore forever involved in a duplicity of reference. On the one hand, it refers to fact; on the other, to mere possibility.

If our logic is constructed to reflect the structure of our actual world (rather than a possible, perhaps even a preferable, world), it will be a logic in which some things are contingent. For even if an entity can be actualized within our particular set of possibles, this potentiality is dependent upon some human or natural actualizing agency, and thus this power is contingent on its action. The actualization of any possible can, of course, appear to be an accident whenever the actualizing power is not seen or recognized. It can also appear to be necessary when that context which it helps to shape is itself considered necessary. Metaphysics grasps necessary and possible actualizing powers and distinguishes between them—or at least that is its primary task if it is to promote clarity.

Possibles which are actualized will tend to take on the degree of either contingency or necessity which is to be found in the framework within which they appear. Considered in itself, the degree of contingency or necessity of any given possible entity will depend primarily upon the degree of steadiness inherent in its actualizing power. To determine contingency-necessity, one must first examine the individual possible in relation to its actualizing agency and next consider this against the factual context in which it appears. This being so, our metaphysical

language will tend to reflect differing degrees of contingency-
necessity depending upon how the individual event is approached.

The basic structure of our world may appear necessary when it
is considered in its context. In fact, it is only contingent with a
certain degree of probability, when it is taken in relation to the
absolutely infinite extent of all possible entities. Theological
discourse often lacks even this form of contextual certainty, since
it speaks about its objects only in the context of all the possibles
considered absolutely. Theological language can exhibit certainty only when it speaks of the rules governing the possibles as
a whole (God), but this does not help it to make statements
which are factually certain. For this reason theological language
can be metaphysically powerful but at the same time appear
practically weak.

If an entity is one among the absolutely infinite set of
possibles, its potential actualization depends upon (1) its
relation to the other possibles, (2) the framework of our
particular world and the rules which govern inclusion and
exclusion, and (3) the degree of power and steadiness in its
proposed actualizing force or forces. The exact expression of this
situation is the business of metaphysical language. Logical
discourse, on the other hand, treats entities merely as possibles.
Logic may treat every possible as such and consider each as a fact
in logical space without regard for the possibility or impossibility
of their actualization within our world. This enables the
language of logic to be more neat and uncluttered than the
metaphysician's exposition can ever be. Theological language has
the even more difficult task of combining logical simplicity
(God's mode of thought) with the more complex and uncertain
language that is appropriate to the actual world (which also,
secondarily, is God's).

It is not possible to think of any entity apart from its context
within the absolutely infinite set of possibles, although we can
consider it in isolation from our (or its) particular spatial and
temporal context. This fact makes metaphysical and theological
speculation possible, and it also accounts for the fact that the
linguistic structures of their expressions are often unusual. If we
can speak momentarily about an entity apart from its context in

some particular set of possibles, still we cannot speak of it apart from the probability of its actualization, and this is why theological language always has causal overtones. Since the basis for its probable actualization is internal to any possible entity, it cannot be grasped or spoken of clearly unless this fact is indicated. Religious discourse always expresses the degree and the power of the actualizing force which it grasps as lying within any entity that is not a part of our actual world, and so it speaks of operations and actualizations which are different from or interruptive of the actual order. Religious language necessarily tends toward the eschatological.

Words may occur alone, but they are meaningful only in the context of some mode of discourse, be it logical, factual (scientific), or theological (speculative). That is because any property of an entity, which is what a word expresses, may appear independently, but it is actually dependent upon the necessary basic metaphysical structure in which it appears. Thus language need not express metaphysics at any given moment, but it is nevertheless dependent on some metaphysical context to establish its basic meaning. Just as any property is a necessary part of all possible sets of possible entities, even when it appears and is spoken of independently, so the momentary independence of all language is a form of dependence. This is true insofar as all language is forced to represent some basic metaphysical structure to establish its meaning.

To know an entity fully would be to know in detail all the possibilities for its occurrence in every set of possibles. For such a task language is actually inadequate, since it is bound by the limits of contextual description. To know in part is to understand the occurrence of an entity within some given set of possibles in such a way that its possible occurrences elsewhere are both suggested and allowed for. For this task language is adequate, but it needs constantly to summon its full powers of expression to do justice to the possible flexibility and not to fall into the common linguistic fallacy of expressing an entity's nature in a manner more rigid than its actual existence. Language expresses definiteness and inflexibility easily; but to express a possible range of occurrences of a possible entity with precision (vagueness being the weak statement of an entity's possible occurrences) is exceedingly difficult, and it requires the exertion of a rare metaphysical power over language.

That such linguistic powers can be exercised is due to the fact that within the nature of every particular set of possibles the possibility of every possible combination is also to be found. As Plato discovered in the *Sophist*, the very nature of an entity involves and is determined by all the possible states which at that moment it is not. The necessary involvement of the force and range of nonbeing in Being gives language its force, its range, its power, and also its problems and its imprecisions. Neither metaphysically nor linguistically is it possible to concentrate upon one entity to the exclusion of all others, nor upon an actual state to the exclusion of possible states. Theologically, language is in fact committed to an attempt to grasp an entity in its setting among the absolute infinity of possibles (the Divine nature) and the powers which establish their laws (the Divine power and will). The difficulties inherent in ordinary discourse are, thus, a special and restricted example of the difficulties of theological language.

Language is an unending process precisely because no actuality is necessarily ultimate. Starting from the accurate description of an actual state, a new possibility can always subsequently be found, and this changes the context in which that actuality is grasped and begins the linguistic reformulation over again. The object remains its factual self, but, since language arises in the area between the possible and the actual, this process of continually discerning a new possibility keeps language in a state of constant reformulation. To know the internal qualities and the possibilities of an object is relatively simple, but, since "to know" also involves grasping simultaneously all the possible external contexts for an object together with its actualizing forces, the knowing of a given object can be relatively simple in the first sense while being metaphysically difficult in the second.

To know all the range of the possibles would be also to know every fact, but the mind has difficulty here, and language is not geared to such complex expression. On the other hand, to know every possible fact, although easier to express, would be to know some but by no means all possible entities. Both knowledge and language can be factually complete while remaining incomplete and inexpressible regarding all possible entities.

Every actual entity also exists in a set of possible entities. I can think and speak about any given entity as though such a set of possible entities did not exist around it, but I cannot know or express its essence without grasping its place within some set of possibles. Since a spatial object must lie in some finite space, the spatial or visual description of an entity is always the easiest, the clearest, and the most amenable to our language structure, as the empiricists have always recognized. Yet since a point in space is actually to be defined as a place in which to consider possibles, any attempt to consider the space in which the object lies (rather than the spatial object itself) will always lead to greater metaphysical difficulties and more complex (if not also less clear) linguistic structure.

Every possible state of affairs cannot be contained within an object; that is too much for any entity to bear. Only an absolutely infinite set of possibles could contain the possibility of every state, although it also contains possibles which cannot exist in any state because of internal inconsistencies that would produce a power failure (i.e., continued nonbeing). Given an already actualized set of possibles (such as our world), the form of an entity is the conditions for its actualization and continuance within that actualized set. An entity, then, is some possible which has become organically capable of achieving and sustaining actual existence. The duration and evolution of this state is a description of the entity's powers in relation to the powers operative in its actualized context. Theological discourse often expresses this as God's activity; metaphysically it may be expressed in less personal terms.

Every linguistic formula applied to complex entities or situations can be analyzed into statements about their constituent parts and powers. Since possibles completely constitute these complexes, any linguistic description of a complex entity necessarily involves language in an attempt to understand all the possibles and their range. Possible entities, it is clear, form the substance of the world which is made up of an organic set of actualized possibles capable of self-maintenance. Possibles, then, are essentially organic entities capable of actual existence taken together with the negative element of those which are not so organically capable.

If the possibles in our world had not come into organic union, a proposition's meaningfulness would depend entirely upon whether it could be located within an absolutely infinite set of possibles. Thus language could be used by, and would be meaningful to, God alone. As for ourselves, we could in that case form a picture of our world as only one possible set and would be incapable of declaring any factual proposition made about it either true or false. Without the actual world as its given base, human language could describe possible states freely, but it could decide no factual cases surely.

It is clear that, however different from our actual world another possible world might be, it must have something—a form—in common with our actual world; in that sense, no possible world is completely unknown to us. This common form is the general structure of the absolutely infinite set of possibles itself. That is, whatever variation of content is possible, no world can escape reflecting its origin by not embodying the general structure which governs all possibles. In this way it is equally possible to learn the general structure of our world by turning away from it and by studying the structure of all the possibles taken together. Or we may learn the general structure governing all possibles by discerning the actual basic framework upon which the possibles in our world appear. Language is a mixed thing, since it can reflect both approaches.

'Substance' means any possible capable of sustaining an actualized existence within some framework. It requires logical possibility, together with some actualizing power, plus a greater or a lesser degree of self-maintenance. Only if some set of possibles had in fact gained an actualized form could there be a fixed frame to the natural world. Yet, considered in themselves, the possible entity, the existent state, and the actualized fact are in essence one. Although they appear in different frames, their origin is one. The existent is the contingent, the variable; the actualized fact is a possible which has become fixed. A configuration of actualized possibles forms the framework of the natural world. Language mixes the actualized fact with possible entities to express the existent state of things.

In the absolutely infinite set of possibles the arrangement is that of a group; some are loosely formed and some are organized within a genus. In any genus possible entities are combined in a definite way, and the way in which possible entities stand together within a group constitutes the structure of that possible class. The form is the possibility that structure has for attaining actualized existence. Any fact has a structure that consists of the form of the groups represented in it, since this form determines how the fact came into existence. Language exhibits such form.

Language and Theory

The totality of the possibles which attain actual existence, together with the possibles which are related to them, is the natural world at that moment. Metaphysical language describes this; theological language gives an account of its origin out of other possible sets; religious language meditates on its future and on its outcome and considers how the introduction of new possibles might alter that structure radically. The totality of possibles which are actual at any moment sets the limits for the actualization of future possibles, the limits of empirical language, and also the range of future discourse. Actualized possibles, together with nonactualized possibles, are reality; and, since this totality is absolutely infinite, language in fact is oriented more toward limited states than toward unlimited possibility. The possible that has come into actual existence we call a fact; a negative fact is the nonactual existence of a possible. Language combines the positive and the negative and is correctly understood when it is grasped in this way, but it is subject to misunderstanding when it is not.

When considered in themselves, possible entities may appear independent of one another, but they are not independent of the set by participation in which they are given definite form. Their independence, however, is such that, from the actual existence or nonexistence of any possible entity, we cannot infer the necessary existence or nonexistence of another, but only its relative probability or improbability. Since possible entities do not seem self-sufficient, when we speak of total reality we mean the absolutely infinite set of possibles plus its actualizing powers or agencies. In that sense, to speak about any reality is to involve language in an infinity and to refer, at least indirectly, to God.

Our mind operates by making for itself designs of sets of possible entities; we speak by selecting out certain possibles and their relationships and sketching them in words. Language, thus, may be understood as the picture of a possible set reflected in linear discourse. Any mental design or verbal theory presents possible entities in some logical order by determining the existence of compossibles and the nonexistence of noncompossibles. Any such structure or theory is itself one possible mode of reality, and the function of language may be described as presenting possible models as more or less actual. What structure any given design has corresponds to and is determined by the set or sets of possibles which it contains. The sets of possibles in the design stand, in the theory, for structures which have or could become real. In this sense metaphysical language is always pictorial; religious language is similarly pictorial, but it is oriented more toward possible structures than toward those which are already actualized.

A theory or a design is distinguished from other statements by the fact that in it various sets of possibles are combined with one another in a definite way so that from it further statements can be deduced and predictions can then be made. Such a design or theory is itself one item among the possibles, so that often it is difficult to tell whether the theory applies merely to possibles or also to actualities. Language too is subject to this uncertainty, and the chief source of confusion comes from an inability to determine what a particular discourse is primarily oriented toward; i.e., toward the merely possible, the partial, or the fully actual.

Linguistic clarity of orientation is difficult to achieve, since a theory or design means a definite combination of sets of possibles in a way in which entities might be related to one another in actual existence. The function of a theory is to exhibit a relationship in which sets of possibles could become actual.

Therefore, in verbalizing that theory (that is, in describing the design serially) it is easy to slip over and to imply that actualities are in fact organized in this way, when they may or may not be or may be so to a greater or to a lesser degree.

Since the mind's natural orientation is toward possibles, when it thinks a theory or forms a picture it may easily hold this in suspension without prejudice as merely a possible form of organization. But when we speak, when we commit a design to words, the theory has in that sense achieved for itself a state of actuality. As it is verbally pushed out into the world, it has a tendency to take upon itself an air of an actual description of actualities rather than of a possible organization of possibles. Thus speech doth make braggarts of us all.

Language commits us to theories in a way in which mere thought never does. In that sense language is akin to physical prowess, whereas thought retains the uncertainty that governs possibility as a whole. Language commits us, just as our bodies commit us to this world; thought withdraws us from commitment, because in its own world it constantly moves among new alternatives. Metaphysical language expresses this situation of thought; religious language seeks to stand between body and thought, between commitment and possibility.

The possibility of any theoretical structure's being in fact the plan of our actual existence we call the usefulness or applicability of such a theoritical design. Thus, the applicability of a theory is the probability that actualized and potential entities can be combined with one another after the manner of the sets of possibles of that outline. In this way any theory is linked with another after the manner of the sets of possibles of that design. In like manner any given theory is also linked with actualized reality, or, more properly: in this way we attempt to forge the link between theory and reality. *Theory reaches up to actuality from possible reality.* Organizing theories is like developing a scale which is graduated from possible reality to actualized existence. As a bare minimum, in order to be a theory at all, a set of possibles must have something in common with the actualized facts which it portrays and claims to apply to. Between the design and the portrayal, there must also be some possible entities (now become factual or potential) which are identical with that design in order for the one to be a theory about the other at all. Fortunately, language is able to express the overlap of one realm upon the other as well as to speak purely internally to a viewpoint.

What must a theory have in common with actualized reality to be able to represent it more or less closely? Clearly the theory must have the same connection (or more or less the same) between sets of possibles that actualized reality has, not some other possible form of connection. In this case, the theory or design can represent every actualized state whose form of connection it has. What we want to know from the theory is what is possible in the world, and that within some forms certain relations and actions are possible while within other forms they may not be. Thus a theory is rendered useless, however intriguing it may be, unless it does contain at least something like the form of connection between sets of possibles that is actually present in our world. A theory or design, however, cannot represent directly its own form of connection with other possible theories; it shows it by being what it is and by the ability of language to ring changes on the theory—i.e., variations that carry it toward related theories. Language, although in itself fixed, in its ability to change exhibits the relations of possibility from which any theory comes.

A verbal picture must represent possibles from without. Its standpoint is one form of connection between possibles. Therefore the theory, being not totally internal to the world of possibles, can reflect within itself how nearly like or unlike it is to our own set of actualized possibles. But the theoretical design cannot place itself outside all possible forms of connection that can exist between sets of possibles; and so, unfortunately, no final theoretical formula is possible. Language, therefore, shows no tendency to stop, least of all to stop itself.

An infinite number of theoretical viewpoints are possible; thus metaphysical language tends to incompleteness and to indecision unless stopped by decisiveness. Only a few of the possible theoretical structures could in fact be related at all closely to our actual world; thus, oddly enough, religious language may be more concrete and definite than metaphysical discourse. Through the definite activity of God's choice, which is what a confusion of tongues. From this the metaphysician must attempt to recover as many accurate ways of speaking as he can.

Philosophy and Language

Philosophy is not able to confine itself merely to the actualized world, although such a wish is bound to be expressed from time to time when we grow tired of unendingness. The object of philosophy is a logical appraisal of our thoughts through a consideration of their degree of possibility. But to accomplish his the philosopher must stand above our natural order. The bject of theology is a logical clarification of God's thoughts ough an attempt to reconstruct the norms operative at the ment of creation. Theology should not be restricted to one icular theory about the divine nature, but rather it should npt to extend itself to understand all possible theories in a way that it can give the best account of the process of ization as it took place from among the infinite possible ilosophy, on the other hand, moves in the other direction; ribes various possibilities but always attempts to add y relating these to the actual order of things. The result ophy should be to make the priorities clear in the way order and structure the various possibilities.

rtially unactualized state, possibles and our thought n become blurred; and philosophy and theology then vork together to make neat delineations. Theology the routes of God's possible actions, and philosophy paths leading to actualization, both past and future. e states include those which violate logical norms, must verge on the unspeakable at times. But when sophy displays clearly in words as much as is ther with an explanation of the reasons for the the barriers to thought. The magnitude of the e extent of what is simply possible is in itself too ngle thought to grasp, which compounds our rything which can be thought of at all can be ccept when we begin to place it in relation to

religious language expresses, metaphysical language is allowed more precision and some momentary singularity of perspective on the infinity of possibles.

Theories and Reality

How is it that more than one theoretical structure seems able to represent reality for us? All any theory must have to exist is the basic form which embraces all of the absolutely infinite set of possible entities and states. Beyond that it may vary from actualized reality by degrees, so that any theory which does not violate the basic form of all possibles is in that sense itself a possible theory. Our task, however, is to determine how closely in fact each one conforms to the peculiarities of the actualized world or how much it merely represents some possible combination of possible entities and structures.

Many theories may be possible, and through them the basic structure of the world can actually be apprehended, but not every possible theory deals directly with our actualized world structure. What we discover is that some metaphysical views are merely compatible with the possibles and can at times depict our particular world, but there is no guarantee that it must or will do this in any particular instance. Thus, existential immediacy—not logical consistency—is really the best way to determine which possible metaphysical view is closer to actuality. This rule we learn from our *Prolegomena*.

Any theory which grasps the basic structure of all the possibles, however, will have at least some minimum common ground with actuality as we experience it. This is what throws us off in appraising a theory, that is if we focus first upon the degree to which it does correspond to some existing structure which is already known. Any theory represents its possible structure as having been actualized, and if the theory avoids internal inconsistency, this certainly might have been the case. The issue is whether the structure which the theory represents was in fact actualized, or whether actually it is only some possible structure with certain similar features. Thus, what we should attempt to do is to assign to each metaphysical theory, both as a whole and in its parts, a degree of possibility measured against what we know to have been actualized. *In an existentialist metaphysics, we now demand (1) that each theory consider within its own framework the degree of probability which it claims to represent, and (2) that it reflect this in its own theory about itself.*

Either a metaphysical theory agrees with our actual world or it does not. Because one entity is a theory, however, and the other entity is a fact or set of facts, it is often hard to be sure of this correspondence. What makes this even more difficult is that a theory may also agree with some merely possible world, and in either instance the theory may make sense internally without determining its degree of correspondence with actuality. Unfortunately for our desire to settle the metaphysical problem, making sense depends not on our actual world but merely upon representing some possible set. The theory is factually true to the degree that it represents the actualized world, but its logical truth merely means that it represents some possible world which could have been actualized. Any significant theory probably contains some of each form of truth, so that our problem is to determine the degree of actuality *vs.* the degree of logical possibility. And this requires some existential material, since from the theory alone it is impossible to tell whether it represents some degree of actuality, or merely possibility. Within the limits of logical consistency, a world of theory is unfortunately sufficient unto itself.

Just as our thought always (if it is rational) corresponds to some set of possibles, so in that sense thought was within itself an actual basis for theoretical construction. And just as our thought in itself excludes no other thought—i.e., sets no limit upon itself—so an absolutely infinite set of possibles is conceivable for our thought. Insofar as our thoughts are factual, their totality corresponds to the actual world. Insofar as we think of every conceivable thought, our thought reaches out toward its limit in the totality of all possibles. Yet even a thought about possible entities contains within itself a consideration of whether the actualization of such a state can be accomplished wholly or partially or not at all. What is thinkable is always possible, although perhaps not always in our particular actual world. We

can even think of a logically inconsistent set of possibles (i.e., v can think illogically), but these thoughts cannot be actuali either in our world or in any possible world, since actualiz demands internal consistency as a condition.

The truth is that God could actualize an inconsisten possibles into a world; his power is sufficient to do goodness, however, restrains him, and it is true that su could not long sustain itself or prevent itself from chaos. God could violate the laws of logic, but it is wise nor very profitable. Language, however, is than God's power and cannot express or commun sets of possibles without considerable difficulty language derives its logic more from our possibles from which contradiction and removed at the instant of creation. Yet f thought in another possible language is en our actual language often seems to this.

That a proposition may represent affairs is often concealed by our or since its oral or printed form o' concrete than it can be in fact. turns out to depend upon the potential state which it descr possibles after their actualiza concrete reference (once a universal *vs.* the particul paralleling our actual w medium, since, if name' least can explore possib'

Individual names construction, but th thing about our w sheer possibility. relation of existe it describes an infinite set of totality of intellect ca'

all that is and to the possibles which are not restricted by logical norms. Words, fortunately, add an even greater degree of clarity than thought can achieve, although we also are sometimes all too aware of the greater depths from which our clear words arise.

Propositions can even represent the whole of all that is possible, but that absolute infinity cannot be presented simultaneously, except as thought symbolizes it and words reflect its intention. Only God occupies the position outside of every possible logic from which point alone the extent of the possibles can be grasped simultaneously, although theological thought does move toward this perspective. How God might have acted in creation we can reconstruct, although our words can never actually show us these events, as they sometimes may in other situations. What can be directly shown need not be said; when we cannot show events, we are dependent on a verbal reconstruction of that possible state. This explains our feeling that we are, at least potentially, actually in possession of every logical conception, even if actually to activate them does exceed our powers. Our degree of power here depends upon the accuracy of our theory of actualization—past, present, and future—both of human and of divine origin.

The limits of my language define the limits of my speakable world, but not necessarily the limit of the worlds of which I can be aware. Logic defines the world of the absolutely infinite set of possibles. The limits of language are tighter than this, but the world of thought is not so restricted. Logic alone, however, cannot tell us what in fact has or can be actualized, but only what might be. Logic merely sets the limits of possibility, whereas theology traces the flow of power as it etches causal chains among the possibles. Logical grounds by themselves (even noncontradiction) are not sufficient to exclude the actualization of any set of possibles. Normative considerations alone determine decision here, plus the limitations placed on power when the agency is man and not God. We can be aware of what defies thought but can express it only indirectly. Thought uses language symbolically to direct attention to what it apprehends but is unable to comprehend or to express directly.

My world is a private world to the extent that language limits expression and logic restricts thought, although in solitude I can be aware of more than I can express or logic will allow. The world in that case really is my world, for in the strictest sense what is most true about the world can only be grasped privately. We live our life on the boundary line between the possible worlds and the actual world, and we cannot always express the relationship which exists between those two worlds exactly as we find it expressed in our own being.

The thinking subject cannot be encompassed in language, Descartes' attempt notwithstanding. For it exists on the border line between the actual and the possible, and these can not be encompassed unless the full range of possibility can be grasped in language. As a subject I do not belong solely to the actual world; I live my life almost more in sheer possibility, although our senses do not lose themselves here but still maintain their contact with the physically real world. My possible worlds, of course, are not all really possible worlds in the sense that our public world permits their actualization, but the limits of my possible worlds (whether internal or external) still define me as much as my actual world.

If we look about in the actual world, where is the metaphysical subject to be located? Everything which we see or do could possibly be otherwise, so that no actual event or set of events tells us a sufficient amount about a subject. The actual cannot be given order a priori, so that it is in giving the actual order its constitution from among the possibles that the subject becomes most visible. The possibles, when taken as an infinite set, have an a priori order, but this never passes over into actual structure or actual experience without the instrumentality of a subject, whether human or divine. When we turn from the actual world and either ignore it or divorce ourselves from it, the self becomes identical with (or perhaps lost in) sheer possibility and tends to solipsism. Actually, to be brought into contrast with simple possibility, can break up our isolation, but such in-between existence is more demanding and uncertain. Some are bound to shrink from it; they prefer to be alone and isolated in sheer possibility.

The self which philosophy seeks is not the man, not the human body, but the human soul describable in philosophical psychology (see chapter 3). The metaphysical subject is the limit of its possible worlds, and to that extent it is not simply a part of the actual world. The meaning of the self and of the world therefore must lie outside the actual world. In the world before us everything is actualized as it is and happens as it does. Yet, the value of these facts lies outside of them, since to be a value means that it must apply to all of the possibles, and thus it lies outside all actual happenings and facts. Value exists between the actual and the possible in their mutual understanding and comparison. Whatever has come to be is contingent, so that value enters in only with the actualizing cause and not with the factual state as such or in mere possibility itself. Unless we comprehend the cause and its relationship to what might have been, we cannot value what is simply because it is. Contrast alone induces value. Value norms are not themselves contingent, since they apply eternally to the possibles, but they become so in relation to a contingent actuality, i.e., they do not have to come into being.

Every ethical proposition thus belongs to some context, that is, it applies to some relationship between the possible and the actual and their intermediary cause or causes. Since all possibles can never be fully expressed, neither can ethics ever be a fully verbal or a final matter. In its existence between the actual and the possible worlds, ethics as a theoretical enterprise is doomed both to contingency and to the same lack of finality that characterizes all of existence. The value norms involved are neither contingent nor subject to change, but the context for their application is. Ethics transcends the actual world, and, just because it does, it eludes fixed expression. The number of ethical norms is actually finite and stable, but the possibles to which they apply are not. This indicates both the fixed and the unstable element in all ethical pronouncements.

Existence and Will

'Will' as a phenomenon of the exercise of power becomes the primary concern of philosophical psychology, and it is the chief reason why psychological exploration comes to have philosophical import, particularly for metaphysics. (This is a conclusion drawn from these *Prolegomena*.) The states and the decisions of will can be charted only as possibilities and never as certainties. Yet, since a knowledge of Being involves a knowledge of the choices which constitute it in some particular form, 'will' is central to metaphysics, and psychological data becomes our most important source of information about it. Good and bad acts of will change the structure of our actual world, although the form of the possible worlds remains unchanged. Those who are unhappy tend to dwell in sheer possibility, whereas the happy are those who are able to live within the actual world, even though the actions of a good or a bad will can change the world and bring certain possibilities to actuality. Given our situation, not every possible can be actualized; hence a metaphysical grasp of the relation of actuality to possibility as it defines the structure of Being is central to ethics.

God's will has been active too, as the actualization of a set of possibles into a world as we know it reveals—in this sense our world is completely contingent and dependent on what is outside of it. The world itself involves no necessary mystery, but how it came to be as it is and not in some other form is a question that involves us in a grasp of the operations of the Divine will. Here mystery cannot be excluded. For one thing, in considering how and why the world assumed the form which in fact it did, we are involved, not with the limits of an actual world, but with the absolute infinity of all possibles. Our reaction to this as an object, in contrast with our actual structure, is the source of all mystical feeling. Here we have difficulty in expressing the theoretical assurances which we may develop, and the questions we ask can be expressed only as probabilities. Yet if the question can be framed at all, it can be given a possible answer, although this is not always one that deals fully and solely in actualities. Any new metaphysics based on these *Prolegomena* must learn both to accept this situation and to deal with it as best it can.

In dealing with 'will' (whether divine or human) and with possibilities rather than with actualities, skepticism naturally is one reaction. Such doubt cannot be refuted, since that can be done only by offering certainties. Yet what we can do is attempt to show why it is senseless to doubt merely because a probable answer is all that is forthcoming. Skepticism is usually based on a desire for a metaphysics of certainty, and so any answer to it can be given only by developing a metaphysics based on possibility and probability. We can show that total doubt is rational only when there is no possible answer. Thus, since at least some reply can be given in response to questions, the proper attitude is, not skepticism, but merely a reaction against the lack of finality. We ought to show that our main problem is to ask the right question in the first place. Too many questions are possible for this ever to be an obvious matter, although some do treat their questions as though they were the only possible ones. But a lack of finality never prevents the asking of a precise question. In fact, precise questions become very important if we are not to lose ourselves completely in probabilities.

Scientific questions can be asked by the natural scientist, of course, with a great degree of certainty, since his immediate object is the structure of the actual world. Insofar as understanding, however, involves us in a knowledge of the possibles from whence our particular structures come, a question of origin always introduces a degree of uncertainty which even the natural scientist is involved with the more he deals with basic structures. The human problems of life are more immediately involved with an attempt to understand the actions of will, and so in this sphere of questioning we tend to move from an understanding of the will's action among possibles and on to a grasp of actuality. The natural scientist tends to move in the opposite direction.

To many, the sense of life at times seems to become clear, but then it fades. How can this be explained? At least partly, this is often due to the fact that insight is oriented toward a merely possible structure. Thus, the insight is genuinely a penetration into a structure of Being, but it is not always into one that either is or can become actual. When this is discovered, the insight tends to fade, since only an insight into the relation between actuality and the range of possibility can be sustained steadily. Insight into either the structure of possibility or actuality in isolation tends to evaporate. (Does this explain the momentariness of most conclusions in the social sciences?) The structure of the actual can be expressed, since our language is geared to it, but such understanding tends neither to be profound nor to be of long duration. When we enter the realm of infinite possibility, we come up against the inexpressible. Thus many return to the actual, in spite of its lack of depth, to attempt to avoid encountering this unavoidable sense of mystery.

Each possible entity is, of course, clearly expressible, but the infinite extent—i.e., the variety of possible combinations and the encounter with levels and structures which are unknown in our actual world—makes expression difficult, owing to the impossibility of simultaneous comprehension or grasp. Man's reach exceeds his grasp, although God's does not, so that for God there is no mystery and no inexpressibility. The theological endeavor is to understand as much from this perspective as our metaphysically trained ability allows us to do. In philosophy we should not attempt to say anything which cannot be communicated clearly, but this of course restricts us to the level of the everyday events of the physical world. In metaphysics, we move away from these restrictions, knowing that to do so interferes with clarity, and realizing that we are talking about merely possible structures, not always actual ones.

Where metaphysics is concerned many have rightly felt that it teaches them nothing about the actual world. We cannot change this, but we can try to indicate why this feeling is correct, and then we can argue that the approach to the actual world via the realm of possibles is the only strictly correct metaphysical method. In theology the correct method draws us even further away from actual structures, since its first consideration is to reconstruct how God might first have moved to actualize from among the possibles. It is ironic to note that here, in contrast with the history of the church, dogmatism is most inappropriate. Our assertions can never represent how God actually did act or what he wills, but rather they can only be a sketch of his possible intent. To a devout believer such procedure is bound to be unsatisfying, since theology in this manner will not seem to tell him anything about God's nature. Nevertheless, this approach to the Divine nature through the action which he takes upon the possibles will still remain the only correct method.

How does a metaphysics (or a theology) of this kind yield any clarity? Propositions based on an analysis of the will as it operates among the possibles (if it uses psychological analysis and literary exploration) can result in possible formulations about Being; i.e., about how it is and came to be and how it might yet be or might have been. Using these theories, it is still possible to "climb up and over" and to grasp the structure of Being without the aid of necessary and certain propositions. We can use one possible theory first to gain insight and then attempt to formulate a more possible theory. We always move in degrees and among a variety of possible theories, never settling merely on one.

Seeing that our option is only among *possible* conclusions, we may be tempted not even to start such a metaphysical construction. But if we will begin, and try to surmount these possible propositions, the reward of seeing the world rightly may await. For Being is a set of possibles which is absolutely infinite in extent, and will controls power to form the decisions which actualize these structures. To Being defined in this manner, a variety of approaches actually is the correct approach; no single avenue can do it justice. Being can be formulated only in a variety of possible propositions, all of which are made visible through various possible theories (about the extent of the possibles and their relation to the actual; and concerning the agency of God and man which operates between both). All these are expressed in various possible metaphysical and theological structures. Such theories are most certainly not all equally true, but one must defend a theory by demonstrating its possibility and by illustrating its virtue through the data for which it can account (for our 'data', see part 1).

As we have explained, even the best theoretical structures of necessity fall short in yielding us a complete explanation. Theoretical and verbal structures do have a certain power but probably not as much as this would require. This means that we sometimes face an inability to speak adequately about the most important issues, and then we may find silence a necessary mode. This need not mean that rationality is altogether abandoned, for it is always possible to explain (as we just have) why silence at any time or point becomes necessary. We can explain the reason for silence clearly, even when that reason is our inability to produce clarity in that instance via an acceptable theoretical structure. This may be due to the variety of possible structures that are applicable in that situation. We cannot always make a direct approach to understanding, but it is possible to explain why a direct approach is impossible. We may sometimes learn more simply by coming to understand precisely why a positive answer is not possible.

Some Conclusions

Have we now proved metaphysics to be possible simply by doing it? Part of the answer given to this question, of course, would depend upon whether the brief *Tractatus* constructed here can be expanded to offer "answers" to traditional philosophical issues. Could it clarify the assertions which were made here only in capsule fashion by a more extended analysis and application? Most often the real test of the usefulness of any view is whether from it new insight can be derived and whether the view can then be extended, expanded, and varied. A good theoretical structure is fruitful in its ability to yield to modification and to produce a variety of subviews. But more than that, if the existentialists have provided the prolegomena for this, a depth of psychological insight should be present, and the resulting metaphysical structure should be not only internally consistent but also fruitful in an ethical application. That a therapy can be provided for our psychological condition (e.g., existential psychoanalysis), and ethical decision then made possible, does not "prove" one metaphysics to be true as against all others. Yet this psychological test and its ethical application does eliminate the merely interesting views which might be applicable to some possible worlds but not to ours.

On the whole, metaphysical views are not fully argued when they are first stated; hence it is not the intent that anything which has been set forth in this chapter should be considered as having been fully explored. Rather, these are exploratory sentences—excursions into the metaphysical realm that has been introduced by the existentialists. They are intended to determine whether this realm exists at all and if so, whether it is substantial enough to support further expansion and elaboration. If a philosopher demands immediate and complete substantiation for every trial assertion, it is unlikely that he will become a metaphysician, however valuable his contribution in another area of philosophy may be. Metaphysics—and its counterpart in theology—demands that speculative extension be carried on until the outlines of the view become clear and its key terms are established. Such an attempt has been made in this *Tractatus*, in contrast with Wittgenstein's earlier *Tractatus*, and this has been done as a first extension of *The Existentialist Prolegomena* into the beginnings of a full contemporary metaphysics.

8

God and Man
As Metaphysicians

The Discovery of Metaphysics

If we want to discover what metaphysics is we cannot start from our own thought. In *Kant and the Problem of Metaphysics* Heidegger attempted to examine and to revive metaphysics through a consideration of Kant's thought. Although others have thought about theology and metaphysics before, it is always possible that any new consideration of the structure of the divine nature might raise metaphysics and develop it directly; but a secondary source for this enterprise always lies in the previous thinkers' writings. The struggle to solve perplexities which are recovered from reading others' works can guide and train our own amateur thought. We need first of all an existing structure—that is, one from which the mind may perceive God—and often the form of another man's thought can provide this. Through such structures we are sometimes enabled to see what otherwise would remain invisible. A stubborn refusal to be dependent in this way, at least temporarily, often leads to the "Death of God" for that thinker.

During the course of his consideration of Kant, Heidegger constantly refers to man's finite nature (see chapter 6, pp. 148–51). This is a fact not so strange in itself, except that 'finite' is a relative term which needs to be contrasted with something not finite if it is to be fully meaningful. That is, we will know man's limit better when we understand and compare it with what God can and cannot do. Finite, for Heidegger, seems to mean that man must react upon objects—that he cannot 'know' without an object's being given to him. If we turn this around quickly, it appears that God's chief characteristic as a metaphysician is that his knowledge is not dependent upon outside presentation. God gives himself his own objects but men do not. Metaphysics requires that human nature transcend itself, that it go outside itself in order to know; but God, to be a metaphysician, need not transcend himself.

Time becomes the crucial category for Heidegger here. Man is not, of course, totally dependent upon other objects. He can solicit, request, seek, and even construct the objects which he wishes to have presented to him. He may alter the structure at points, but he does not cause the context to exist, nor does he cause the conditions and the alternatives themselves to come into existence. Whatever his powers of alteration may be, every presentation and every metaphysical analysis is still pervaded by time. God, on the other hand—although he is temporal insofar as his mind follows creatures and the created order—stands above time as its creator, and this is a role which no man can play. To the extent that man is free, God's knowledge is limited by and subject to time's outcome for its completion. And yet, it is still true that God constituted the temporal order and freely subjected himself to its partial limitations, whereas man was born within the fixed temporal frame and transcends it only when, as metaphysician, he turns to consider God's ways.

Were it not for time, human beings could neither be nor function. God does not require time in such an essential way, but, having freely created a specific temporal order, he must subject himself to it to know its outcome. God is subject to the temporal order for knowledge of its detail; its framework and its possible combinations he knows eternally, since he selected them in the moment of creation. God transcends his eternal nature in knowing time; man partially transcends his temporal nature in knowing objects other than himself. And man can leave even the temporal realm (but only to find it reflected there once again) in his attempts to determine the structure of the divine nature. Truth comes from the disclosure of other temporal beings to us.

Truth about the temporal sequence itself comes when the divine nature is discerned or disclosed. Truth comes for God in the decision involved in the moment of creation.

When we seek to grasp the structure of the beings which are presented to us, we discover the need for an orienting ground and for a context within which to understand another object and its relationship to us. Only the general structure of Being itself can provide this; therefore, at least a covert grasp of (and thus a potential knowledge of) Being itself is also grasped in the knowing of any object. Yet Heidegger stops the reflective process one crucial step too early. The general structure of Being itself also requires an explanation, once it is discerned. For suddenly the metaphysician cannot be sure whether the structure which he has grasped is the actual structure of the world or whether it is only some possible structure of being which is close to but not identical with the actual one. To decide this, and thus to be sure of his general interpretive framework, the metaphysician must ultimately turn to God—i.e., tend to become a theologian—to discern something of the divine structure. If he can reconstruct the divine activity in creation, perhaps then he can determine whether the structure of being which he has grasped is the actual one or whether it is simply a possible—but for some reason rejected—plan.

As finite beings we can receive only what offers itself. God determines what can possibly offer itself to us as an object, although he does not set the details of what in fact does. God can receive any possible object without the object's offering itself. The totality of all objects possible in our world he knows through his creative choice, but even God can receive the actual object only when it offers itself in time. For God, the "unknown" is the detail of actual events; the absolute totality of possible temporal structures he knows nontemporally. Man's unknown is the future—until it is presented—as well as the totality of all that is possible which lies behind the present structure.

Man needs metaphysics because he is finite. He grasps a general context whenever any being is disclosed to him; and, if he explores this in the attempt to know the fundamental structure more explicitly, he has become a metaphysician. God needs metaphysics because the details of the actual order were created with certain indeterminate factors involved. Thus, God grasps the general temporal structure as the framework within which to place the changes wrought by man's decisions. Man as metaphysician is sometimes wrong; that is, he grasps a possible structure of Being rather than an actual one. God is never mistaken about the structure even when temporally he is uncertain about some specific outcome.

Earlier and more fundamentally, God was a metaphysician in order to consider the totality of the structures of Being which were possible, and next he was a metaphysician in willing the creation of one of these into an actual form. Fearing his ability to make a mistake, man attempts to check the general structure which he has grasped and to determine whether it is actual or merely possible. He becomes a metaphysician later, just as God did originally. He becomes a metaphysician in attempting to trace the grounds for God's creative selection of one structure over the others which were equally possible but differently attractive.

From Metaphysics to Theology

Any metaphysician can avoid theology, but, if he does, he can never be sure how close to the truth his apprehended structure is. The "fundamental metaphysician" must become a theologian to determine just where his metaphysics stands between those structures which were possible and those which became actual. God was the metaphysician in creation which man must now become. Man is the actualizer, and this requires that God now become a temporal metaphysician too or miss the facts. On the other hand, man as metaphysician must become a theologian in the attempt to check the accuracy of his particular metaphysical scheme.

Since time is oriented toward the future, man's nature is necessarily future-oriented in his search for understanding. Yet, in order not to be lost among the possibles, man must also grasp the past and its specific origin. His nature makes him a metaphysician of the present and of the future; the solution to his metaphysical task requires that he understand God as metaphysician—i.e., that he know the constitution of the past and its original alternatives. Our orientation to the future gives us our imaginative capacity; our reference to God gives us our stabilizing and our actualizing capacities. Human subjectivity lies at the heart of the metaphysical problem and defines it; only a knowledge of God's action and a grasp of his nature as a metaphysician are capable of solving it. By being man, he is required to become a metaphysician; to complete his task, he must next be a theologian. That is, he must trace the divine activity in its original creative constitution of Being's structures.

Man's finite nature requires a constant questioning of himself, both of his nature and of his capacities. To answer these questions in the context of a knowledge of the structure of Being in general is to be a metaphysician. God's nature requires no such constant questioning of himself, but his knowledge of the actual activities of man does require that he constantly question man, that he understand human metaphysics. To discover an answer for his constant questioning, man would need to become a divine metaphysician; i.e., one who selects and determines the world's actual structure. Both his nature and this constant questioning require of him that he gain some knowledge of a being who is not finite—that he become a theologian in theory.

If finitude involves freedom, as well as limitation and being surrounded by time, then even God requires metaphysics as a theoretical basis upon which to comprehend both his own and human freedom. Metaphysics now becomes a joint divine-human enterprise, although God is not subject to the problems of finitude from his own nature but, rather, only through his knowledge of ours. Metaphysics, although intimately associated with time and limitation, arises in God chiefly because of man's freedom and God's conscious attempt to understand this freedom. In man, metaphysics has an unconscious origin, since every man feels a desire to understand the operation of finite freedom within himself. In moral man's dilemmas this becomes a pressing problem, and, for the metaphysician, it becomes a conscious enterprise. He must look back toward the structures of actual Being and uncover God's original work in forming them.

Both man's freedom in action and in thought force him to transcend himself and to attempt to understand his own finite nature and the structure of being within which he operates as these two work together. Unless forced to transcend both the structure and himself, man cannot find self-understanding. Understanding requires a grasp of the origin of the structure and a realization of its origin in God and of how man is related to his given structure in a manner that is different from God's role as a creator and a selector. Both God and man achieve understanding by creating theoretical structures which then exist external to their basic nature. When these structures are comprehensive enough, they are metaphysical; God always understands within a metaphysical context, and man sometimes does.

God constantly exists as a metaphysician; he embraces eternally within his own nature all possible theoretical structures, yet produces only one. God respects Plato's Parmenidian One to that extent. Man is forced to transcend himself and sometimes to become a metaphysician, both because of his nature and his desire to understand what springs from it. Man's theories, however, still lack the singularity which is possible only for God. We may and often do attempt to repeat God's singularity of choice, by which he elected one theoretical structure, but we are never able to sustain such unity for very long. Man seeks to govern himself theoretically by the One, but he does not have the power to do so fully. He seeks theoretical unity, but he is forced to accept a definite multiplicity.

Man constantly drives toward this desired singularity of metaphysical structure in his theoretical endeavors, whereas God is driven by man's freedom toward a greater multiplicity of theoretical structure than the stability of his nature would in itself demand. In becoming a metaphysician of man's free action, God forecasts possible outcomes. He is always sure of the basic structure within which these choices are made—a certainty that is unavailable to man.

God is uncertain about the specifics of human action, although he originally chose the framework that allowed human freedom. Man's uncertainty about future action is compounded by his metaphysical perplexity over the basic structures within which his will is free to operate. God constantly must renew his metaphysical activity as creator in order to know man; man's metaphysical task must constantly be renewed so that he can determine the structure within which he operates, its possibilities, and its limitations. To understand that structure more concretely, man seeks to acquire a knowledge of the God whose choices first established it.

The Ongoing Task

The human metaphysical task was and is and ever continues to be. It is the essential freedom within the divine nature which makes continued theorizing both possible and necessary. If God had not been free to construct our basic metaphysical structure from among the possibles, metaphysical structure would necessarily flow from the divine nature, just as Spinoza thought, and our thought could rest more secure. The ebb and flow of theoretical structure, the constant rise and fall of new interpretive structures both scientific and metaphysical, the feeling of openness toward new theoretical frameworks which are not yet formulated—all suggest a basic freedom and flexibility in God's original act of structuring. And it also indicates that there may exist a fluid boundary between our actual structure of being and all the possibles from among which God chose freely. The evolution of philosophical thought, far from being necessary, is explainable only by the assumption of God's original freedom and flexibility in fixing the structure as one which now reflects itself in our never-final metaphysics. Metaphysics of necessity is a free enterprise. The attempt to fix philosophical thought in any one mold amounts to an attempt to bind God's creative powers in a way in which he has never yet bound himself.

Human finitude, at the same time, does make the construction of metaphysical theory possible. It is a necessary function, and yet it is one never to be completed or established as certain. Were we as men not subject to limitations unknown within the divine life, we should not construct theories but simply live. But the freedom of God's original metaphysical choice now reflects itself constantly within our practical life. Thus, men act neither without perplexity, nor without thought, nor without ultimately constructing theories. Freedom demands theory as a guide; uncertainty requires theory in forming decisions; and so our limitations and freedoms together tend to make metaphysicians of us all.

We theorize to support the decisions which we find to be necessary to us and also in an attempt to introduce theoretical stability into our situation. Once formulated, a metaphysical theory can add an element of stability and clarity, but this is so only momentarily. Because more than one theory originally was open to God's choice, a metaphysical proposition can always suggest a variation on its own theme. The degree of stability that any theory is able to produce is primarily due to the formulator of the theory and to his success in holding to a single perspective.

The stability of any theory is derived neither from the basic metaphysical reality of an absolutely infinite set of possibles nor from a God who was (unlike us) unrestricted in his original power in constituting a metaphysical framework from among them. Metaphysical stability in theory originates in and is produced by the individual metaphysician. To induce such stability is the ultimate test of our powers. If we bind God to the theoretical stability which we produce (as some metaphysicians seem to insist on doing), we confuse the difference between God's role and ours as metaphysicians.

God's omniscience allows him to hold every metaphysical view in one perspective simultaneously. All are related firmly, through his will, to the actual framework which he originally selected, and in this enterprise he is dependent only in the sense that he must continually formulate a new theory about his relationship to human freedom as man develops. Man's limited intellectual range necessitates constant revision, extension, and inclusions. All this is forced upon God by man's uncertainty and because of his free decision whether to become a metaphysician or not. As a result, man is sometimes as unable to finish his task as he is to become God. Man can make the possible combinations of all possible entities hold still momentarily so that they take on the form of a metaphysical theory, and in accomplishing this man mirrors in thought only what God's actual power was in the act of creation.

Some Conclusions about the Divine Nature

What must God's nature be, if he is to be aware of change and time and understand them in their full temporal sense without being, himself, essentially temporal? This need not mean that God's mode of knowing is atemporal, as has sometimes been argued, but his nature must include the changes which produce time, and his understanding must be able to follow them without this characterization of his own mode of being. This is not the traditional eternal knowledge of temporal things, but it is a way of allowing God to know temporally without being temporal himself.

Like man in knowing God, God requires an understanding which can grasp modes of being not its own, as they are and without reducing them to himself. If man's understanding is the power to assume the form of its object without losing its identity as understanding, then God's knowing could assimilate to change, novelty, and contingency and assume their form in understanding without being like them in nature. God could know temporal events as they are without reducing them to nontemporality or necessity and without being temporal himself except in that sense of knowing.

Kant has shown that we cannot even draw a line or move along it without generating time. Does God, then, generate time in knowing the various relationships among the possibles in his own nature or in grasping in knowledge the contingent outcome of temporal events as sketched above? To consider the latter situation first: in following the course of those aspects in man and nature which are contingent and free, God does generate time in his understanding, but it does not cause movement in his nature, as it so often does for us. Not always or necessarily, but on the whole, our motion is generated by time as time is generated in our understanding, even when its object is so motionless an entity as a number or a geometrical form. God's nature is powerful enough to hold firm against the tendency to motion which the temporal movement of understanding produces. He may yield to it and act, but he may also hold his nature immune from the effects of time.

Even granted that God may know contingent events temporally without necessarily having time infect his nature, what about the more difficult question? That is, as God contemplates the absolute infinity of possibles, in themselves not even bounded by the law of contradiction unless it is imposed; as God contemplates these and their possible combination, does his understanding generate time and does time in this situation invade his nature? We have already indicated that God (as traditionally conceived) can take even the infinite, timeless, possible relationships between all possible entities simultaneously into his knowledge. Still, his knowing generates time within itself, since it accommodates itself to the possibles, and their nature is to assume connections in time to the degree that their actual existence is also possible. But these objects are internal to God's nature. Does this special situation (the internal relationship) generate time in God's nature as well as in his understanding?

It does, in the sense that God is detached from the events actualized in time. Unless he intervenes, his relationship is simply that of accommodating his understanding to their contingent action. In his own nature, however, he is not detached from the possibles, so that a knowing of them and a calculation of their various combinations for existence have a tendency to set his nature in motion, but his will and power are sufficient to contain this. He may release the motion, since his knowing generates it, but he is not forced to, and he may hold his nature aloof to motion if he so desires.

Now our original question returns: Is man capable of a similar knowledge—not nontemporal in its generation in our understanding but only in its grasp of entities not themselves temporal and in our ability to grasp them without introducing motion and time into our nature? Yes, but not with the element of perfect control which God exercises. In conforming to nontemporal entities, our understanding generates time in the knowing of them, and most often the motion involved affects our nature. Yet at times it need not. Our mind moves as it follows relationships between possible entities not in time; and not always, but on certain occasions, our understanding may move but our nature will be held motionless in its grasp of nontemporal entities.

As we have argued, this is made possible primarily by the inbreaking of nonbeing. When concentrating on the modes of being, the release from time does not seem possible, since all these have entered into the temporal sequence. God, in contemplating the possibles, is more aware of nonbeing than we, and in that sense he is more released from time's motion. We are first impressed with the modes of being in time, but gradually certain events open our mind to the range of the possibles, or certain crisis experiences (such as facing death) bringing our mind up against nonbeing. In his relation to the modes of being and nonbeing, God tends to be silent, since speech requires motion in time. We speak in relation to the actualized modes of being, but when we face the possibles and the force of non-being, our speech is at least reduced. When threatened in its existence our mind stops, and then we grow silent. And, if we allow our minds to move, we may learn while our nature is stopped in immobility and gain understanding while our tongues are motionless.

Heidegger has given some attention to modes of being other than "dasein"—i.e., modes which are not necessarily this or that. If some mode of being is considered ultimate, whereas that of a mathematical entity (or dasein) is not, we can see at least a degree of release from temporal structure. Not-being—i.e., everything a given form of being is not—cannot be in time, as dasein is. In fact, its very nature is that it is not involved in the temporal sequence, as existence here and now is, and yet it is real. To focus on this is to see only one part of being as time-locked. Although the understanding generates time in knowing any mode of being or not-being, the effect is different on the knower when the entity known is not itself in the temporal sequence. To know ourselves as we are illuminated by nothingness, to see our nature against all that it is not and its possibility not to be, is to know ourselves as not essentially in time.

Are alienation and anxiety the crucial experiences in which we are most forcefully aware of our temporality? Yes, that certainly is our first impression; but we have argued that these also are the experiences which can release man from temporal bondage. How are both results possible? When nonbeing confronts us our anxiety (or our alienation from self or others) makes us aware of the time-locked nature of our being. But to the extent that nonbeing opens possibility to us, we can then discern entities which are not in time, whether they are possible to our being or merely to some theoretical system. We are aware of our temporality as contrasted with all that is possible but that is not actually in being. Then, we may brood on our temporality, or we may be released from it into the not-being of the infinite possible modes of being, the confrontation with which first produced our existential crisis.

We exist in process and in question, but when the question is radical enough, process stops and questions are suspended. This is precisely because we see that they were based only on our mode of being and must be reorganized to include all of not-being. To put our being in question reveals its temporality, but to stop it with the thought of death (or to confront it with all that it is not) is to point up its nontemporal core. From this experience, the self swings either toward being stopped in time and bound to one moment, or toward release from temporal modes and toward a knowledge of time's limited applicability to all that is possible but that is not. Thus, time has a limited application to God and to knowledge which is not provincial in its scope. Being which is beyond what is this or that is not in its essence temporal, although the mind in knowing it may generate time in the movement of its grasp. "That time is generated whenever we think" is not the same as "that all thought and all possible entities are temporal." The shock induced by confrontation with nonbeing can freeze us to time or point up this fact, or it can release us from time's total dominance.

If we have 'being' as the absolutely infinite modes of all possible being, which includes a majority of nonbeing (modes which can never be) ; and then if such entities are themselves nontemporal (except as the mind generates time in considering them and their possible relationships) ; how is it possible for them to be connected as events in time? The first part of the answer to this crucial question is that in themselves these entities are defined by the possible connections which they may or may not have with one another in any possible context of time. What cannot be connected out of time because of incompatibilities cannot connect events in time, and some of our failures are due to a failure to recognize when this is true. Those whose nature as possible entities relates them in certain possible ways to other entities and to modes of nonbeing, can also be so connected in time, although only with the degree of contingency and variety allowed. Of itself, no possible or class of possibles enters or is connected in time. Will and power alone can add actuality, so that the connection of events in time comes about because the nature of possibility basically allows for it; but more importantly, it is because will commits the power of actual existence to them.

In following the connection between events in time, then, the mind may be aware of the addition of power given to the modes, and it can then consider them as they are connected in time. But when properly blocked from its preoccupation with actual being, nonbeing and sheer possibility can free the mind to consider all modes of being and non-being as just what they are and not necessarily as they are in time. When we do this, we follow a mode of thought which God used in selecting a world from among the possibles for creation. All abstract thought, whether in physics, mathematics or metaphysics, follows this form, although it is never in pure separation from time, as God is able to separate it. When we can see precisely where and how and when and under what conditions time does and does not enter God's understanding or his nature: in such a moment of insight—perhaps opened to us by crisis—God's nature can be seen and man's nature clarified. The philosopher's reaction to this is to speak as precisely as he can; God's reply is silence. Time does not dictate to him, and he does not have to talk his way out of bondage.

The Nature of Metaphysics

In summary: Metaphysics is not a structure in the world, but a human activity; i.e., an activity which uses the structure of previous metaphysical theories as a basis from which to extend its explorations. Man as metaphysician cannot stand alone or construct from nothing; he builds only upon and from previous theories of the nature of things. Only as thought works against thought can insight come. Here God and man differ as metaphysician. To gain insight into the structure of things, God needs no thought other than his own to work against. At the moment of creation God needed the power of decision in order to elect one structure for actuality and to hold others as merely possible. In comprehending man's free action, he needs to learn man's decision process so that he can know the paths which men take as actual rather than as merely possible beings.

Man as metaphysician needs objects and also thought other than his own against which to work; his insight is not given to him but instead must be won through repeated effort. Because man is not God, he continually discovers new possible structures. Just because he does not know but must always reconstruct God's decision in creation, man is never certain whether what his thought discovers is an actual structure or merely a possible one which God considered but rejected in his original creative action. Against this setting (i.e., being neither blind nor possessing full knowledge), man makes his free decisions. Then God as metaphysician follows man in his creative activities (only some of which are successful), while man seeks to separate the actual from the possible structures by reconstructing God's original decisiveness.

God stands above time, but he is oriented toward it in his knowledge of man's free action. Man transcends time only as his decisions help to determine its direction. To that extent, an encounter with nonbeing forces man as metaphysician to construct and to reconstruct a theory of the divine nature and its creative action. God freely subjected the actualizing of a portion of his knowledge to the outcome of man's behavior, and yet he still stands above time as its creator. Man exists only in time, except insofar as he becomes a metaphysician of the divine nature and its activity. God as metaphysician creates the temporal process and observes its course; man as metaphysician begins within the temporal order. Occasionally he adds to its specific actualization; and, as metaphysician-turned-theologian, man by means of theory climbs to view the process as God does. God's creative grasp is sure; man's speculative grasp is always subject to uncertainties. He is never finally sure whether he has in fact seen the actual structure which God first elected or whether he has merely grasped a more or less closely related possible structure.

By being man, and therefore being oriented toward the future (see chapter 6), each of us must become a metaphysician in order to understand. We must see the past and past theories as material for our thought. To complete this metaphysical task, man must next become a theologian; i.e., attempt to trace the course of the divine activity in its selection of our actual structure from among the possibles. By being God, God too must be a metaphysician; he must see a knowledge of theoretical structures as a means for understanding man's free action. God could have avoided his partnership with man as metaphysician had he not elected one set of possibles for actual life and, more than that, had he not selected a structure in which some free actions remain possible. Man, by nature of his subjection to time's process, is forced to be a metaphysician; God became one through his power for free, creative selection. God became a metaphysician of time and freedom because he elected an order which is still capable of flexibility.

God controls uncertainty, as its creator. Man reflects uncertainty in his never ending theoretical construction and in his psychological states and in his literature (see chapters 3 and 4). Until man can duplicate every possible that is known to God, until he can connect these with the criteria involved in God's creative decision, his metaphysical endeavors can never stop but will continually be forced on by lack of final comprehension. At times and at moments, man's theory will seem to intersect God's line of action, and precisely at these points his theory will become illuminating and his words will yield insight (at least to some). His lack of full control may force man's theories off the divine path, and then our words become dull, unilluminating— possible but not really related closely enough to the actual to be insightful.

God's metaphysical activity, freely undertaken in his original decision not to create a completely necessary system, focuses his metaphysical attention on one small corner of the wide range of his vision of an absolutely infinite set of possibles. God's attention is on the moments of decision in which men actually break through to freedom. God has made himself an observer, a metaphysician, a knower of men—just as man's uncertainty makes him a metaphysician, a knower of God through constant theoretical reconstruction. Man is a knower and a not-knower driven on by uncertainty and sometimes even by despair.

All this, of course, assumes that metaphysics is a possible enterprise and a structure which man has within his powers to create. Although philosophy has never been without its skeptics, it was primarily Kant and his successors to the present day who called metaphysics into question on epistemological grounds. If, as I began by suggesting here, a contemporary metaphysics of possibility can best be built by contrasting and thus by coming to understand the role of God and the role of man as metaphysician, it is still proper that some attention be given to the Kantian critique. Although metaphysics can never be built out of epistemological considerations alone, it is true that the discovery of new epistemological material might in itself suggest fresh insights for metaphysical construction. With this aim in mind, the existentialist epistemology and psychology should be thoroughly examined for their metaphysical consequences. It is this process for which these chapters are prolegomena.

Epilogue

Retrospective Understanding

In philosophy it is often true that understanding comes only in retrospect. In line with the existentialist dictum that existence precedes essence, we should "work our way through" the problem presented, in this instance metaphysics, and pause only *after* the conclusion to see whether it is, in retrospect, now clear just what we have done. An existentialist basis for metaphysics does not yield us one and only one valid metaphysical view, but we should at least be able to look back over our explorations and list the criteria by which we may now test the validity of any proposed metaphysics. This should be done by reference to the empirical base uncovered by existentialism in its literary and psychological explorations. And, in line with our argument that metaphysical questions themselves undergo change, we should (after the conclusion if not in advance) be able to formulate the major metaphysical problems of our own time.

In his *Philosophical Fragments* Søren Kierkegaard (S.K.) has a section near the center simply entitled "Interlude." In a similar fashion, before attempting any retrospective summary, we should pause and gather our strength for the task in our own "interlude." As we indicated in the Prologue, this actually is an example of what is first being last, since S.K. is the first of the existentialists, and yet Sartre and Heidegger (not to mention

Wittgenstein) have provided most of our examples so far in this essay. As we mentioned, this oversight was intentional, for Kierkegaard has less to say on conventional metaphysical topics than the other authors whom we have used as sources. It is true, however, that his "Interlude" is perhaps the most valuable small piece in existentialist literature concerning a metaphysical revival. And at the same time, we can deduce from it the major features of an existentialist-based metaphysics.

Suffering and Necessity

It is interesting that Kierkegaard, who usually has little to say about metaphysics, and even considers himself anti-metaphysical, should suddenly stop in the "Interlude" and consider 'being' and 'becoming'. What is it that occasions this sudden metaphysical excursion? Although entitled *Philosophical Fragments*,[1] that short work actually begins with a consideration of Socrates and of truth, but it quickly moves on to devote itself primarily to a reinterpretation of the central features of Christian doctrine (e.g., the suffering servant, miracle, faith, etc.). That this should be the context for one of S. K.'s rare excursions into abstract metaphysics points up the fact that existentialist insight comes in the midst of very human and sometimes personal (in this case religious) considerations. These can at the same time serve as an immediate base to give a concrete anchorage to the abstract considerations. Turning away from what S.K. considers to be Hegel's abstract metaphysics, Kierkegaard himself finds in the center of human concerns an insight into a new metaphysical form.

What is the insight which S.K. gains in considering metaphysics in this context, and what does this tell us about the form for a contemporary metaphysics? In the first place, it is important to note that Kierkegaard begins with Becoming (p. 90); then, reversing Plato, he uses this as the standpoint from which to understand Being. Moreover, S.K. uses 'suffering' as the key concept for the understanding of Becoming, and this places

---

1 Kierkegaard, 2d ed., trans. Howard V. Hong (Princeton: Princeton University Press, 1962). All page references in this section are to this volume.

metaphysics in the context of existential psychology. Any plan on coming into being is changed in passing from not-being to being, and the source of this change is the 'suffering' which all coming-into-being involves. Since what is necessary does not suffer, the change involved in the coming-into-being of any plan thus argues for the nonnecessity of all Becoming. In analyzing Becoming to understand Being, we discover freedom.

Becoming, therefore, is never necessary (p. 91), and all becoming takes place with freedom, since the suffering involved in the process of coming-to-be will exclude necessity. If we had overlooked the suffering involved in existence, we might think that Becoming was a necessary process. The approach to Being, however, via both Becoming and our psychological explorations focuses on suffering and also reveals Becoming to be, not necessary, but free. This leads Kierkegaard to consider the 'past' and the 'historical', which are the famous loci of Hegelian metaphysics and are also the centers of tremendous energy since his time. We are fooled, S.K. concludes, when we interpret Being through a study of the past, for the past does not admit of change once it has come to be what it is. Thus, it gives the appearance of immutability and necessity. Whenever we concentrate exclusively on the past, we tend to forget that its apparent immutability was first brought about by a change. If the past were originally as necessary as we sometimes take it to be, we could not distinguish past from future, but in fact we do.

Instead of beginning with history, the past, and Being and then understanding the present, the future, and the process of Becoming on this basis, Kierkegaard bids us reverse this and focus first on the phenomenon of suffering in the process of becoming. This induces change into any plan as it comes to be, and it leads us to interpret Being and history in terms of freedom. A generation engaged in understanding the past, as we have been, does not like to be reminded of the future (p. 96), for there freedom and uncertainty are less easy to overlook. Because it is no longer in process, the past can give us the appearance of necessity, but what we must do is learn to apprehend the past, not as it now appears, but as it was when it was still future.

The historian who understands this priority of becoming over being and who approaches history with this new metaphysics must act as a "prophet in retrospect" (p. 99). When we use the future as the basis for interpreting the past, and not vice versa, we discover the 'suffering' which becoming undergoes. This will disclose to us that the apparent certainty of the past is in fact based upon an uncertainty, ". . . an uncertainty that exists for the past in precisely the same sense that it exists for the future, being rooted in the possibility . . . out of which it could not emerge with necessity. . . ." (P. 99.) If a historian sees his task thus transformed, he will come to feel again a passionate sense for becoming and wonder; it would never occur to a man to feel 'wonder' over a necessary process. Now that such uncertainty is seen to be attached to all the apparently certain events of history, it recalls the philosopher to his traditional passion of 'wonder'.

Thus understood, the historical comes to have the same elusiveness that is implicit in all becoming, and we might have missed this had we taken the past at face value. Uncertainty can now be seen as present in the past too, and this makes it, not a subject for certain knowledge, but a proper object for belief only. The "new historian" who views the past in this light will find that his mind is in a stage of suspense, exactly as the mind of a contemporary would have been. A contemporary of the events could not have predicted them with certainty, and neither can a later historian who understands the process of becoming. Toward this, the only proper attitude is belief, not knowledge (p. 104). It is, then, no easier to try to understand after the event than before—a thesis that strikes at the heart of an era of historical research which hoped to find in history a basis for certain understanding. History is robbed of its special standing by the existentialist analysis. It is put on a par with the future insofar as certainty is concerned; that is, when we understand Being through a prior analysis of the uncertainty of Becoming.

The actual is always different from the possible, since suffering must induce at least some change in the process of becoming-to-be. Thus, the actual cannot be conceived with certainty in advance. Viewing historically, we tend to overlook this and to transform the actual back into the possible once more. Kierkegaard had been considering the problem of the distance between a Christian disciple in a later era and the locus of his belief in a historical age, and this was what first led S.K. to reconceive the relation between Being and Becoming.

Both past and future tend to become unreal when conceptualized, but now the suffering known immediately in the present process becomes the interpretive anchor which prevents us from considering the past a necessary set of events. The historical is nonbeing to the extent that it lacks existence, so that an existentialist analysis of the present qualities of existence (e.g., suffering, freedom) must be added to the historical to restore its reality. The nineteenth-century confidence in historical understanding has been based on a misunderstanding of existence, and this is something which now must be taken as ontologically prior. In a few sentences S.K.'s analysis brings two centuries of historical effort and confidence to a halt.

Kierkegaard had not trusted metaphysics, because he took it to be unavoidably historically oriented. He thought that it had to take necessity as its standpoint and therefore could not give an accurate picture of the contingencies of present existence. Analyzing existence psychologically gave S.K. a new basis for understanding Being through the categories which were derived from Becoming, just as previously the path of understanding had moved in the other direction. To do metaphysics had not been his intention, but suddenly the analysis of the religious difficulties of the "contemporary disciple" led to a new understanding of Being and to a way of reintroducing into historical understanding precisely that element of contingency and wonder which had been lost. The historian now must first know the uncertainties of the prophet, and then he will see that both of their enterprises are embraced by the same contingency. Thus a new metaphysics of Being appears, although it is not at all clear that S.K. recognized it as such.

Theology also undergoes reconstruction here, since it follows that God must also suffer and undergo change and experience contingency, if he is to enter into becoming. Kierkegaard remained conservative and traditional in this theology, but still he provided an insight which is capable of launching a theological revolution in our understanding of God's nature. What could be more important than this for an age that has lost its ability to think about God systematically? In the *Concept of*

Dread,[2] S.K. had also set the stage for a new metaphysics, although he did not actually bring it forth. Again, what we have there is a meditation on a religious theme, this time 'sin', and this is explored and is to be understood on the basis of a psychological exploration of 'dread'. What is disclosed here is the centrality of 'contingency'. To explain the constant presence of dread, we discover the pervasiveness of contingency, and now we must revise our idea that Being involves necessity.

Kierkegaard's analysis of dread comes out of his discussion of sin (here is psychology serving as a basis for theology) : S.K. interprets innocence as ignorance and ignorance as 'nothing'; hence dread arises out of the discovery of the nothingness which innocence is (p. 38). Dread grips us, and, having arisen from innocence, it can now cause us to fall from that state (p. 39). Dread is ambiguous, both attracting and repelling man, but it serves as a catalyst which is capable of moving man from mere possibility into some actuality. Yet again, the analysis of the fundamental quality of dread argues against necessity, since there would be no dread involved in the fall into sin if it were merely a necessary process (p. 45). This experience of dread reflects our apprehension of our basic freedom in the face of the nothingness of our innocence. When we gaze down into our own possibility, we experience dread as the dizziness caused by the realization of our freedom. In the face of this realization we often fall (p. 55).

The Theme of the Argument

Using both the "Interlude" from the *Philosophical Fragments* and the *Concept of Dread,* we can hope now to see better what this Prolegomenon has argued. Spurred on to consider Becoming, in working out the problems which a contemporary Christian faces and in analyzing dread as the cause of sin and then in exploring its causes, S.K. discovered a new interpretation of Being which uses Becoming and nonbeing as the basis of its

2 Kierkegaard, trans. Walter Lowrie (Princeton: Princeton University Press, 1946). All page references in this section are to this volume.

analysis. Contingency and freedom must be put back in history, and this is done by using the future as the model for understanding the past and thus robbing history of its apparent necessity. Dread as a psychological state can be understood only as an apprehension of a freedom which is basic in the very structure of Being. Dread is not something to be overcome, as Spinoza thought. Instead of being a misapprehension of Being, the pervasiveness of these psychological states actually indicates that they are a reflection of the constitution of Being itself. *Mental instability could not be unless Being were such as to be able to induce it in those who lose control of freedom.*

Here we find support for the theme of chapter 8: that Being is such that both God and man must be metaphysicians in order to cope with it, although God's nature is essentially different in that it never allows a loss of control. We should be able to see now why chapter 1 asserts that the existentialists have (perhaps unintentionally) made a new metaphysics possible, and why in chapter 2 we begin to unfold what special qualities such a new metaphysical knowledge might have. To agree to such a revived and revised basis for metaphysics, the data on psychology and literature offered in chapters 3 and 4 must be accepted both as empirical and as usable now for philosophical appropriation.

Chapter 5 attempts to indicate how abstract knowledge now can be derived from an empirical ground. Chapters 6 and 7 begin the new metaphysical construction, chapter 6 by indicating how the analyses of 'nothingness' and 'time' have become our two central contemporary concepts. Chapter 7 goes about this by sketching a metaphysical scheme which takes this existentialist material as its guide in structuring its concepts and accepts the new insight into the structure of Being which existentialism has abundantly provided. Kierkegaard began this metaphysical revolution, but his concepts led to such different results that he could not carry them out; and he either could not or would not recognize his analysis as a new basis for metaphysics in immediate experience, which is what Kant required.

Are we now in a position at least to describe the basic features of such a new metaphysics? A detail of exact doctrine would be against the spirit of Prolegomena, but the problems considered and the form of the consideration can be outlined now and will still leave variety and flexibility. First of all, contemporary metaphysics can no longer be wholly historical and oriented to the past. The existentialists have announced an end to the age of history. Not that history will be ignored—far from it—since metaphysics can only build by using previous theories. But we will use the experience derived from an orientation toward the future as the basis for understanding the past, rather than use historical understanding as the model for every other form of knowledge. We will interpret the present by its second side: the future. In theology God's divine plan can no longer be found in history but can be located only in the future. Eschatology, then, is the key contemporary theological issue. Any understanding of God in history is also distorting in its image of his nature, but the future reintroduces freedom and gives us a new basis upon which to understand God's nature. On such a basis perhaps God can be made to "come alive" again.

Freedom, it follows, becomes the major problem which should characterize contemporary metaphysics now that the bond of necessity in history has been broken. As long as metaphysics insisted on necessity, the problems concerning the control of freedom were not paramount. Now, in a nonnecessary structure, the crux is to be able to give an account both of freedom and of the means for its directed control. Necessity is a connection between possible states, and as such it exists in thought alone. What comes into actual existence suffers the changes of contingency; necessity nowhere exists actually as such. This the existentialist analysis of experience has now revealed. Many, of course, have discovered that experience does not yield necessity, but usually this has been connected with or has resulted in a metaphysical skepticism. The psychological experience of the existentialists is of a different quality from sense experience, and so perhaps it can lead to a new understanding of Being where the empiricists have failed.

Revolutions in metaphysics have, of course, been proposed by many others before us. These, however, are prolegomena to a metaphysics, not the doctrine itself, because all we wish to see is whether or not the existentialists have in fact succeeded in providing an empirical base for metaphysics. It would not be difficult merely to develop new or revolutionary metaphysical views, but the excitement which comes from the existentialist prolegomena arises over the possibility of finding some ground in immediate experience as a basis for this speculation. Is the data of the existentialists unique, in that it is at once immediate and concrete and yet yields insight into Being itself? That is, is it of such substance that it can guide metaphysical exploration and also test its results? These are the metaphysical questions of our day, bequeathed to us by an existentialist psychology and literature.

Metaphysics and Health

If we can at least outline the general nature of this new metaphysics and the problems which will become essential for it, can we also support our empirical claim by providing at least some criteria to test the validity of any new metaphysics which may be developed? Since the new metaphysics springs at least partly from psychological analysis, it should be such that it is capable of some depth of psychological penetration. Its words should be powerful enough to yield insight into man's inner life. We know that some words are more powerful than others which seem to be equally logical, perhaps because the former are closer to the actual structure of our world as it has come into being. The power which words have to penetrate should indicate the closeness of that view to the actual nature of things, whereas the lack of force of certain other verbal formulas indicates, not a lack of possibility, but simply that that structure was not in fact ever made actual for our world. Here the work of "existential psychoanalysis" provides valuable supporting evidence.

This leads us to ask about the ethical connection which a contemporary metaphysics seems to have. A metaphysics, however intriguing and consistent it may be, should be able to yield ethical advice of some profundity; otherwise, we know that it perhaps applies to some other world, not to ours. This helps us to distinguish the probable from the possible metaphysics, and then the more probable from the less probable. Of course, it is true that many others before us have connected metaphysics and ethics (e.g., the Stoics and Epicureans) , but the point here is that the existentialists have given a psychological insight into man's experience which is of a different basic quality, and it is to this that a new metaphysics must be ethically related. A new ethics should flow from the new metaphysics, which now is psychologically based.

The movement of existential psychoanalysis is still too new to be appraised, but it is this kind of connection which a modern metaphysics ought to seek. Philosophers at their best have been in the midst of the problems of their time. They provide various theories upon which issues can be dealt with, and they believe in the practical applicability (indeed necessity) of such philosophical theory. Plato's vision of the union of the philosopher with the king does not seem to be very strong as an ideal today. Yet Plato often used the physician as his example, and it could be that the new physician—the psychiatrist—just might join the philosopher to form a new ideal: the metaphysician-physician.

In another era the art of physical healing might have seemed to be illustrative, as it was for Plato, and yet perhaps no one thought that it had any systematic relationship to philosophy. Since some physicians have now turned to the art of healing the mind, it is possible that philosophy and this branch of medicine can find some actual point of union. There are already some attempts to do this. Perhaps this explains the odd position which Freud and Jung seem to occupy. Clearly they are both new stars in the theoretical firmament; but still they do not seem to be empirical enough for medicine, and yet they are too metaphysical for a skeptical generation of philosophers. If, then, the existentialists have provided an empirical base that can now attract philosophers to renewed metaphysical construction, we might provide a ground upon which to understand both Freud and Jung as theoreticians of a new metaphysics. Moving philosophy back toward ethics in this way, its motto might again become that of Epicurus in the *Fragments*. "Vain are the words of a philosopher which heal no suffering of man."

Index